I Am Not My Hair

✦

A young woman's journey and triumph over breast cancer

Tyesha K. Love

iUniverse, Inc.
New York Bloomington

I Am Not My Hair
A young woman's journey and triumph over breast cancer

iUniverse books may be ordered through booksellers or by contacting:

iUniverse
1663 Liberty Drive
Bloomington, IN 47403
www.iuniverse.com
1-800-Authors (1-800-288-4677)

Because of the dynamic nature of the Internet, any Web addresses or links contained in this book may have changed since publication and may no longer be valid. The views expressed in this work are solely those of the author and do not necessarily reflect the views of the publisher, and the publisher hereby disclaims any responsibility for them.

ISBN: 978-1-4401-9172-5 (sc)
ISBN: 978-1-4401-9173-2 (ebook)
ISBN: 978-1-4401-9174-9 (hc)

Printed in the United States of America

iUniverse rev. date: 6/14/2010

Dedication

This book is in dedication to and in honor of the women in my family diagnosed with cancer:

Martha Jennings - Great Grandmother (Deceased)
Joyce Kidd - Grandmother (Deceased)
Norma Burger - Great Aunt (Survivor)
Irene Wimbush - Great Aunt (Deceased)
Marnita Kidd - Mother (3-time survivor, BRCA1 positive and author of "Strong on the Inside")

I dedicate this book to my children, Taylor and Joseph, to help educate them on their family's medical history and teach them how to be proactive with their health. I hope they may be able to educate their children and their children's children.

This is dedicated to all of the men, women and children affected by cancer and the caregivers that dedicate their lives to caring for them.

I Am Not My Hair is also dedicated to:

Betty Garland – Shan's Aunt (Fighting Survivor)
Linda Corley – Family Friend (Fighting Survivor)

In memory of Lillian Hall – A new found friend. A friendship cut short. You will always be in my heart and I will forever cherish my "Hope" ring. "Onward & Upward!"

Foreword

Reading Tyesha Love's description of her experiences with breast cancer was especially powerful for me, an oncology social worker who for 12 years provided emotional support to people and families dealing with cancer. Maybe it was reading Tyesha's journal and entering her personal world; perhaps how vivid her experience seemed when put to paper. Most significantly, I responded to Tyesha's frank and intimate portrayal of what it is like to have cancer - uncertainty and fear mixed with tears, laughter and love, as well as physical, emotional and financial upheaval.

So many people who have been diagnosed with or affected by breast cancer tell me that they feel lost and disconnected from others, and from their lives before cancer entered. Knowing that they are not alone is essential, and the way in which Tyesha invites her readers into her world provides reassurance that she, and many other women before her, have been able to find their way. I imagine that all of Tyesha's readers - including women impacted by breast cancer, their families, physicians and healthcare workers - will be as struck as I am by Tyesha's vibrancy, honesty, determination and her capacity to give and receive love as she experienced the life-altering nature of living with breast cancer.

- Stefanie L. Washburn, MSW, LSW

A true, bold, and courageous telling of her-story, Ms. Love reaches to the depths of her pain, not knowing if she could push through to see another day, another hour, and at times even another minute. Just as the many women before her who have heroically fought this fight before, Ms. Love has emerged as a modern day heroine, vulnerably exposing her pain and challenges. I invite everyone to read this story of raw truth, survival, and victory.

-Tamarah Ynise, Author

At some point in our lives, we will all come to experience a life changing moment. "You have breast cancer," are words that transformed Tyesha Love's existence instantaneously. Tyesha captures this season of her life through striking and unedited accounts of the effects this horrible diagnosis had on her world.

Perhaps the most difficult task for me, as caregiver, was my daily reminder to Tyesha of how much her children need her – here; now; with them. Through strong faith and the love of family and friends, Tyesha tackled breast cancer head on; oftentimes with photos of her children in hand.

This is a remarkable book and journal rolled into one. Tyesha outlines her bout with no holds barred. Not once does she vituperate breast cancer. She plowed through her treatments and surgeries and grew to respect the disease. As will you, after reading this extraordinary work. Her recollections will leave you more knowledgeable and sensitive to those who battle or have battled breast cancer and survived.

- Deidre L. Rountree, MS (Caregiver)

Acknowledgements

I want to acknowledge those who inspired me to make my journal public in order to be a testimony for others. Deidre (Shan) and Michele, you really pushed me in this area as I hesitated with exposing so much of myself.

Tamarah, I appreciate you taking time out to offer tips on preparing my book, publishers, copyrighting, and getting it published. Your insight means a great deal to me. Also, your words and expressions, regarding my book, spoke volumes. Coming from you, I am now elated about my "Courageous Experiment." I am so much more comfortable about opening up to the world about my experience after your influential, inspiring words, and accolades.

Shan, thank you for helping pull the title together. I appreciate your dedication and motivation in helping me carry this out. I also thank you for the role you've played in making this a journey to share.

My dear Aunt Pat, thank you for believing in me enough to carry this out, and for celebrating it before it was even completed.

Norma (Aunt Mopie) Burger, although it was a distressing experience, it was a pleasure going through it with you. Our lunch, On-Demand horror movie, and "swill" dates were spirit boosters for the both of us. I love how we've bonded through all of this.

Tyra, thanks for the photo shoot that produced this cover page. You have *"Creative Eyes."*

To Ben H. and Kurt W.: Thank you for taking the time to prepare my manuscript for publication. Your skillful edits ensured the professionalism of my work while retaining the essential elements and integrity of my journal. I am moved by your support and enthusiasm. You're the best!

Special Thanks

First, I want to thank God for seeing me through this ordeal; for not giving up on me. Although I had some difficult times, I kept the faith and did my best to leave it all in His hands trusting that He would see me through.

I want to thank Deidre (Shan) Rountree for dedicating all of her time and energy into caring for me. God couldn't have sent a better caregiver (angel). You have been there through it all, seen it all, encouraged me, lifted my spirit, cleaned my wounds, handled my medical business, financial business, accompanied me to appointments and gave me unconditional love and support. I am eternally grateful for all you have done and for all you are. I'll love you always, my dear friend: my personal cancer-patient-care aficionado.

Thanks to my family for all of your prayers, love, care, concern, support and encouragement. You let me cry when I needed to cry, you kept me laughing (the best medicine), and you helped give me strength in my weakest moments.

My dear friends; all of you know who you are (named throughout this book)...Thank you! Thank you for lifting my spirits, visiting at just the right moments, jumping through hurdles for me, supporting, encouraging and praising me. I am blessed to have each of you in my life. During this season, I learned what it means and what it feels like to have true friends.

To the Church of Christian Compassion (CCC), St. Peter's Lutheran Church, St. John's Lutheran Church, Andrea Wyche (discipleship teacher) and discipleship sisters at CCC: Thank you for keeping me spiritually grounded; for lifting me up and encouraging me. Thank you for all of the visits, gifts, prayers, blessings and support. I love you.

The firm. I couldn't have asked for a better place of employment to support me as you have. I can't thank you enough or express how you've moved me with your support and encouragement.

My professors and classmates (Cohort AA005 and ORG11) at Eastern University, thank you for all of the prayers and inspiration.

Thanks to all of the organizations (named throughout this book) that have been a blessing in the lives of my children, caregivers and me.

Introduction

My journal started out as therapy for me. It was to be used as a reminder of what I endured and how far I've come in each stage. Many began telling me that I could help a lot of people if I shared my experience. I was hesitant to expose so much of myself to the world. And then I thought, *how selfish of me. If this is my purpose, to be a testimony for others, how can I keep this to myself?* So, I chose to share my journal for those faced with breast cancer in hopes of helping them to make decisions based on real experiences. I wanted to give insight to survivors, caregivers and loved ones on how serious this disease is and the changes a plight, such as this, can put one through. This disease does not just affect the stricken. This disease affects all those involved in the lives of those afflicted.

These are my experiences of some of the emotions a survivor feels; thoughts a survivor has; decisions a survivor must make and some of the obstacles/challenges a survivor will face. This book is not to be used as medical advice. I am not an expert in this matter and everyone's battle is different. It is simply my opinions, thoughts, perception, and personal experiences. This is still, my memoir, my therapy, my memento.

Brace yourself for my journey as a single parent of two; full-time student; full-time employee, who was diagnosed with cancer at the tender age of 29. Strengthen your awareness and build empowerment from the revealing account of my true story.

Some contents of this journal are graphic.

As I find myself overwhelmed with some of the things going on in my life; feeling like the world is crashing down on my shoulders; like I've lost control of everything, Shan says, "Meek (from my middle name Kimika), what did Bush do when that fella threw his shoe at him? He ducked, right? Sometimes when too much in life is thrown at you, you just gotta duck."

March 1, 2007 Gene Test

I met with Meredith, a gene specialist at Abington Hospital. Because of my family history, it was highly recommended. I tested positive for the BRCA1 mutation. I acquired the attitude of, *"Yes, I have the gene but that doesn't mean I am going to get cancer. It simply means that I am at a higher risk for developing a cancer."* I simply wanted to live my life as if I never heard the news.

The information I received, goes a little something like this: As I have not had breast cancer, as a carrier, my chances of developing breast cancer by the age of 50 goes from 2% to 33-35%. My chance for developing ovarian cancer by the age of 70 goes from .05% to 6%. My chance of developing pancreatic cancer by the age of 80 goes from 1% to 2-4%.

BrcaAnalysis is resourceful for information regarding gene testing. It compares the percentages of cancer development between the average person and someone with the BRCA mutation. I received two pamphlets: *"Beyond Risk to Options"* and *"What can you do when breast or ovarian cancer runs in your family?"* http://www.BRCAnow.com/

October 10, 2007 Mammogram & Ultrasound

I have an appointment for my annual mammogram and ultrasound at Methodist Hospital. I have been getting mammograms since I was 25 years old. My family doctor and gynecologist strongly suggested it, since cancer is so prevalent on my mother's side of the family. The mammogram was negative; however, the ultrasound found a small lump on the right side. They said it's benign. They did not discuss removal of the lump so I am going for a second opinion at Chestnut Hill Hospital. My Aunt Norma, who was recently diagnosed with breast cancer, referred me to Dr. Bailey. My aunt speaks highly of her bedside manner and her proficiency.

October 30, 2007 Second Opinion

Went to get a second opinion from Dr. Bailey. She did an aspiration, drained fluid from the lump, and confirmed that it was only a cyst.

However, because of my family's history, she highly recommends that I get an MRI as it gives a three dimensional look at the suspected area(s). She referred me to the University of Pennsylvania. She says they specialize in the technology and readings of MRI's.

November 21, 2007 The Lump

I went for my MRI at the University of Pennsylvania. A lump was found in the left breast.

December 6, 2007 The Lumpectomy

I had an appointment with Dr. Bailey about the lump found in the left breast. They gave me a numbing medicine and cut right into the breast around the areola, a biopsy. I lie there feeling the pulling and tugging, but not much pain. I tried to remain focused on Dr. Bailey as she tried to distract me from the discomfort by talking about the kids, the holidays and humor of loving, dysfunctional families. The site grew sore hours after the biopsy. An ice pack and some Tylenol helped.

Although I knew the results would not be available immediately, my heart raced and my palms were moist with sweat as fear overtook me. I tried to remain positive and calm myself by refusing to claim the worse.

December 10, 2007 The Diagnosis

I was at my workstation when I received the call from Dr. Bailey at Chestnut Hill Women's Center. "Tyesha, I'm so sorry, it's cancer." My world stopped, the walls at work began to close in; I fell to the floor, crying. *"It's a mistake; she has to be reading the wrong medical chart. Double check the records! You made a mistake!"* All of these thoughts went running through my mind. She asked me if I was alone and I told her I was at work. She apologized saying she would not have told me had she known I was at work. She called my cell number thinking it was my home number. She remained on the phone with me in silence. I could not stop shaking; crying. After a few moments, Dr. Bailey told me to follow-up with her in two days so we could discuss my options for surgery and treatment. After I hung up, I didn't know who to call, if I could call anyone.

I felt delirious. My mind was clouded. It felt like I was thrown into a nightmare. The day no longer felt real. I couldn't believe what I just heard. I took a few deep breaths and managed to call Kelly, my co-worker and good friend. She sat by my side, crying, trying to comfort me. She told me I had to call my mother. With trembling hands, I sat on the floor; knees pulled into my chest. I made several failed attempts to dial my mom. When I finally got the keys on the phone right, she answered and I couldn't even speak, but the silence told her everything. She lovingly told me that it will be ok. She asked if I called anyone. Told her she was the first and that I couldn't call anyone else. After talking on the phone for some time, she said she would inform the family. The calls and emails flooded in. I couldn't respond to the emails, I didn't answer the phone. I was overwhelmed with emotions. Anger at God, frightened by the news, and comforted by the loved ones that reached out to me.

I pulled myself together and tried to continue on with my day as usual. It felt like I drifted off into a nightmare.

I knew people loved me. But that day, I realized just how much I meant to people; how significant I was in the lives of others.

One phone call in particular was Sherell's. We have been friends since elementary school. As we got older, we went on and had our lives: going to college, having children, getting married…but we maintained our friendship through the years talking only here and there. It took her a couple of days before she called me after getting the news about my diagnosis. She said she just broke down and couldn't call me until she got it together. She said she knows we do not talk everyday, but our friendship is forever; she's a root in my life, and not a leaf. She said she is willing to do anything to be here for me. She gave me encouragement, offered her support, love, and prayers. Our conversation went on for about 40 minutes or so of her professing her friendship, love and support. All I could do was cry. I was moved by my long-time friend's raw expression of emotion. Her reaction and expressions was completely unexpected. She warmed my spirit bringing me a moment of peace and comfort at such a tumultuous time.

December 15, 2007 Dear God – Trying to Give it to Him

Dear God,

Have mercy, Lord. I am terrified. I am terrified of having to endure such a challenge. I am angry, scared and nervous. I have spoken to family, vented to friends and it does bring a temporary comfort. I am coming to you, dear God. I need you to be with me as I face these fears; this challenge. I ask you to help me with acceptance, guidance, comfort and peace. I ask you to help me build my faith and trust in you. Help me to give this all to You, put it in Your hands so I do not carry these worries. I give it to you Father, that You see me through this.

I give you my worries. Please strengthen my children and guide them during this season in my life. I want you to take control of this and help me to accept and deal with the path that has been laid for me. I am putting my trust in You that You have a handle on this. Thank you for being my Lord and Savior and for your grace and mercy.

In Jesus' name…Amen

December 17, 2007 Starting my List of Questions to Ask the Oncologist

- What is the status of my receptors (estrogen, progesterone and HER2)?
- What treatments (regiments) will I need, how many?
- What foods should I avoid?
- What are the common risks and side effects?
- What can I do, if anything, to reduce/manage side effects?
- How concerned should I be about premature menopause?
- What lifestyle changes, if any, should be made during treatment?
- How long does each radiation session last, if I need radiation?
- How do I prepare for treatment?
- Is there anything I should avoid before, during, or after treatment?

December 19, 2007 MRI-Guided Biopsy, Meeting the Oncologist

There ended up being two lumps that were found in my left breast. After the biopsy, a week later they had to do an MRI-guided biopsy on the second lump to relocate it and run tests to find out if it was benign or malignant. This was another rough experience. They laid me face down on the bed, stabled my right breast, almost like getting a mammogram but not as bad, pricked me with needles to numb the breast, put me in the machine (MRI) for pictures, took me out, cut into my breast to take samples, put me back in the machine…this went on about four more times. I couldn't understand why I was feeling discomfort in the front top of my breast if Dr. Schnoll was working from the side of my breast. Then I realized that was how long the needle was.

The actual biopsy wasn't painful. I did experience some discomfort, but the emotional part of it was the most distressing. I lay there wondering, *"Why me? Why am I going through this? What's going to happen? Can I beat this?"* I lay there struggling with my faith and confidence. It's a very trying experience as fear, doubt and concerns of the unknown ran rampant through my mind.

I just started praying to God for peace and comfort, over and over, as the anxiety overtook me. Next thing I know, I was awaken by the nurse telling me they were finished.

I did suffer a bit of bruising a couple days after the MRI guided biopsy. An ice pack and some pain medication helped.

The results from the MRI guided biopsy on the second lump… benign.

When Dr. Domchek, the oncologist, walked into my room, I saw a younger face than I had expected after hearing about her reputation: experience, skills. She exuded confidence and knowledge. I could tell she was aggressive with the treatments of her patients. I liked that she gave off an air of passion for what she did. She spoke to me about the different chemotherapy regimens and the lengths of time for treatment. It's possible I could get a treatment every two weeks for three to four months. She told me about the side effects with chemo and the medication to help me with some of the side effects.

December 23, 2007 The Significance of Taking Notes

It seems that during every doctor's appointment I go into a zone. It is important to have someone attend appointments with you, take notes or bring a tape recorder as you will forget half of the things that were discussed. There is so much information to absorb while your mind is off in a zone. My mother, children and my dear friend and caregiver sat with me during my first meeting with the doctor about the diagnosis. All I could think was, *"Why is this happening to me? This must be a dream. Wake up!"* If it weren't for the notes Shan took, I would not be able to recall what was discussed.

December 27, 2007 Tests

The chest x-ray, bone scan and blood work were not what I expected. I just stood in front of an x-ray machine and had pictures taken. The dye was injected for the bone scan. No stinging, burning…nothing. I lay down, fully dressed, and the machine scanned me from head to toe taking pictures.

The results from the chest x-ray, bone scan and blood work were negative.

I cannot believe how expensive these tests are. I saw the statement for the blood work, bone scan and chest x-ray; everything came to a total of $4,004.70. Thank God for insurance.

December 28, 2007 Thanks via email for the Gifts from Bianka, Duck, Anthony, Michael, Shan, Dad, Tamarah, Lisa, Candice, Nini

I should have known something was going on. My sister rushed upstairs to my room, bags in hand. I could hear her fumbling around in my bedroom, but didn't think much of it. She later calls me to my room. There's music playing and wigs aligned on my dresser. She hands me a card that left me trembling and in tears as we embraced.

"Last night, Candice presented to me, from all of you, a beautiful CD of uplifting dedications, an inspiring card and three stylish wigs. I cried…I cried hard. I was moved by the love, support and encouragement.

I thank God for each of you. I thank you for all you are in my life. I couldn't have asked for a better support group.

I do what I can to keep my spirits up. I know that I am strong and I am ready to take on this battle…and win. When I have my moments of doubt, sadness, anger, fear…it's moments like this, moments you all give to me, that lift my spirits and put me back on a positive track. Thank you for being the blessing you are in my life."

I love you dearly,

Ty

January 12, 2008 The Night Before the Sentinel Node Biopsy

My mom, Candice, Shan and I had a glass (or two) of Riesling and watched *Rumor Has It,* eating as much as possible before midnight, last night. We discovered the positive way is to look at it as "Eat as much as you want before midnight," instead of "I can't eat anything after midnight". Stuffing my face surely distracted me from my anxiety. However, it's 4:53 am and anxiety is kicking back in, and I started to toss and turn, so I figured I'd grab the laptop and start journaling.

I went into Chestnut Hill Hospital yesterday for pre-admission, which consisted of paperwork (medical history, allergy checks, etc.), blood work (which they did not do since my records were current) and blood pressure check.

My little girl easing my worries with an embrace

January 13, 2008 Sentinel Node Biopsy

It was a long day Friday. I arrived at the hospital just before 6:45am. Carey, the nurse, did paperwork, took my blood pressure, temperature and walked me through what the day would bring. The anesthesiologist came in and put an IV in my left hand. At first, I didn't care for his stoic demeanor, but I was able to get him to talk about his line of work and he opened right up. That helped me to relax.

I was taken to radiology to meet Rebecca who prepped me for my dye injections. Dr. M. injected me in the breast four times to administer the dye. This required four needles to the nipple area. It was an extremely painful stinging as the dye was injected into my breast. All I could do was cry and hold tight to the bed to keep from jumping up and running out of there. Dr. M. kept stopping, asking if I wanted to take a break before the next shot, asking if I was ok. I told him through heavy panting and thick tears that I wanted to get it over with. After the last shot, he wished me well and told me to hang in there.

I had to wait two hours for the dye to take effect, so I was brought back to my waiting room and sat with my mom, Candice and Shan. I had to massage the nipple area every ten minutes where the dye was injected to make sure it worked to its fullest capacity. They kept teasing me, saying it looked like I was feeling myself up. Got jokes?!

At 10:00 am, I was brought back to radiology where Cindy scanned and printed pictures of the site where the dye was injected. I was then brought back into the waiting room. Amanda, the social worker at the Chestnut Hill Cancer Center, stopped by to see me. She kept us laughing which helped take the edge off after the experience I had with the dye injections.

At approximately 12:30 pm, I was called to go into the OR. Reality set in. I felt like I was being rolled in onto the television set of ER. They laid me down on the bed, spread my arms to secure them, and said they were going to inject something into my IV to relax me before they gave me the sedative. They attached the monitors, cleaned the site to be operated on and injected the sedative. I was asleep before I knew it.

Eight lymph nodes were removed. **Results:** All clear!

I woke up groggy, in pain and anxious to see my family. The medical staff made sure I could hold down some crackers and white cranberry juice. They explained my discharge/post op instructions and I was on my way.

The first night was uncomfortable. I was in pain, nauseous and lightheaded. Shan took great care of making sure I had enough food in my stomach to take more pain medication. She made sure I was comfortable and helped keep the house in order. My mom and Candice looked after me as well and saw to it that the children were taken care of. This was a huge help as I could only focus on what I was going through. It still seemed like a nightmare and I was finding it hard to accept my diagnosis.

Tamarah and Will were my first home visitors. It was good to have them over. Talk about comedy. They lifted my spirits. My dad came the next morning. We prayed and talked. It was comforting bonding with my father on a different level, cancer bringing us even closer. El visited that night, Saturday, for Chinese, movies and wine. All of my company have been great distractions from what I've been dealing with and what lies ahead of me.

The University of Penn home care nurse came out Saturday morning. She removed my bandage, checked the incision site to make sure I was clear from infection, did some paperwork and told me the signs to look out for: fever, increased pain, pus, etc.

By Saturday afternoon, there wasn't much nausea from the anesthesia and the dizziness had ceased. I was able to get out for a minute to see my classmates at Eastern University's beautiful campus; got Chinese food and went home to rest. It was a beautiful day to get out. Being in the sun and enjoying the positive company of others does something wonderful for the spirit.

Since I had the sentinel node biopsy done on the right side, I must take special care of this side. I have to do exercises with this arm to make sure I don't lose mobility or develop lymphedema, a condition of localized fluid retention caused by a compromised lymphatic system. I can no longer have blood pressure or blood work done on this arm. I also have to use deodorant only. No antiperspirant. It must be aluminum free. I tried several brands: Tom's of Maine and Arm & Hammer, but the ones that seem to work best for me are Adidas and Herbal Clear.

January 15, 2008 Letter to Family and Friends. It's Official.

Friends and Family,

It's official. This is happening and it's happening fast. My last day of work will be January 28th, and then I will be out on medical leave. My surgery is scheduled for January 29th at Chestnut Hill Hospital. I will be in the hospital for a few days (3 or 4 at most), then I will be home.

If you want to check in for an update, please call my sister Candice at xxx-xxx-xxxx. I will be answering my cell phone a day or two after my surgery. For those who want to visit, please allow me the first day/night to rest. I know I will need this. I look forward to seeing all of you any time after that. I should be back online about a week after my surgery. So if you want, send me an email.

For those of you that I failed to follow up with, my bone scan, blood work, chest x-ray and sentinel node biopsy results came back NEGATIVE! I actually got the results from the sentinel node biopsy today, so I had a great start to my morning. God is good. I will not, as of now, need radiation, but I will need chemo. Hopefully, I will not need too many treatments since everything is looking so good right now.

You (my family, my friends, my job) have been so supportive and it really helps my spirits during this time. I couldn't have asked or prayed for a better support group or medical team. I have really been blessed.

All my love,
Ty

January 18, 2008 Nephew Gabriel, A Baby's Intuition

I sat at my kitchen nook watching my sister straighten up after dinner. I rested my elbow on the dinner table, my mood...pensive. My one-year-old nephew walks over to me, finger pointing out and up at my breast. As he neared, his hand finally reaching my breast, he blew a kiss. I just held him and cried.

January 20, 2008 The Breakdown

Chills, shakes, crying hysterically. I just collapsed on my bed crying uncontrollably. I bottled up all I have been feeling since the day of my diagnosis. I pasted on a smile to get through the day as if none of this was going on. Balled into a fetal position in the middle of my bed, I allowed myself to feel the fear of the unknown of what lies ahead for me. I felt the fear of surgery, reaction to chemo, how this would affect things in my home, my children, relationships and friendships. I felt the world was crumbling from beneath my feet. A full blown migraine set in, the nausea started and the irritability began. I couldn't move. My mom called and talked to me for a half hour about the struggles of battling cancer and the rewards for withstanding the fight. She told me to cry, scream and do whatever I needed to do to get it out of my system. I had to allow myself to feel what I was feeling. I had every right. "But, when you are done," she said, "take every piece of clothing off; get in the shower like you are starting your morning. Wash all of those emotions, that heaviness, down the drain. Lotion yourself down, put on a fresh coat of makeup; a fresh spray of perfume; a new outfit and start your day over." She told me she loved me and said she'd check in later.

I did exactly as my mother said. It felt like a weight was lifted off of me. I was completely refreshed after getting all of that out of my system and started my day over. Thanks ma.

January 23, 2008 Starting the Transition. Cutting My Hair...

Sandy, my hair dresser, cut my hair today. I decided that I would play with it before chemotherapy took it away from me. So, I colored it two weeks ago and decided to have it cut for my last week of work. I went from approximately 15 inches of hair to an inch of hair in the front (curls) and shaved low on the back. I was trying to do a cross between a Nia Long and Halle Berry haircut.

I could feel the hair falling down my neck as she cut. It slid down my shoulder, back and then onto the floor. I sat in the chair while Sandy chopped away and allowed myself to have a silent cry. When she told me to look at myself in the mirror, I broke out in tears. I loved the new look, but despised what it signified.

January 23, 2008

THIS BLANKET
*THIS BLANKET WILL PROTECT YOU AND KEEP YOU WARM,
THERE IS NONE OTHER LIKE IT WITH SO MUCH CHARM, IT IS
MADE WITH MY LOVE FOR MY FIRST BORN DOVE, A TREASURE
TO CHERISH IN IT, EACH TIME YOU SLEEP IN IT, SO WRAP
YOURSELF UP NICE AND TIGHT AND REST YOUR SOUL FILLED
WITH PEACEFUL SIGHTS, ALTHOUGH THIS BLANKET WILL
NEVER BE YOUR MOM'S ARMS, KNOW THAT I PRAY YOU SAFE
FROM HARM, REMEMBER YOUR MOM LOVES YOU, SHE'S AT
PEACE KNOWING LIKE THIS BLANKET GOD ALSO COVERS YOU...*
MOM

Wrapped in the Quilt Mom Made

January 24, 2008 My New Look

Of course it drew attention at work. They loved my new hair style, but wondered why I cut off my long, thick, beautiful hair. I simply said, "I will be losing it to chemotherapy." Mouths dropped, words escaped lips, and eyes filled with sympathy. Many offered referrals for second opinions, not wanting to believe it, especially because of my age. Some offered their support, prayers and encouragement and the others simply broke out in tears and embraced me. It has been an emotional day telling those at work what I was about to endure. All of those days I longed to have a break from work. *Ugh, I need a vacation. I need a break from work.* Everyone looks forward to a vacation, a long weekend or a small break from work. But not like this. "Careful what you wish for," they say, "You just might get it." Be specific when you ask the Lord for something. *Lord, I'd like a ten day vacation in the Bahamas so I can enjoy a nice break from work.* Oh well…

January 26, 2008 "Feel Your Boobies" Evite

Any reason to have a get-together, right?

You must wear something pink. If you do not have something pink, throw a white shirt in the wash with something red. Bring a C cup bra (in celebration of my new jugs) or wear a wig (in support of my new do). I'm not doing anything big, as most of you are used to. I figured a couple glasses of wine, some laughs and some take-out. Keeping it simple, but wanting to have a bit of fun before I am a shut in. Would like the company of my loved ones to lift my spirit before the big day.

We'll have the big party when all of this is over with. It'll be a victory & graduation party (Yes, I'm still going for that degree).

I am truly looking forward to seeing all of you this weekend. Please be reminded that this gathering is for all of us to mingle, socialize and unwind. We'll share laughs, smiles and celebrate life. Hope to see you there.

Love Ty

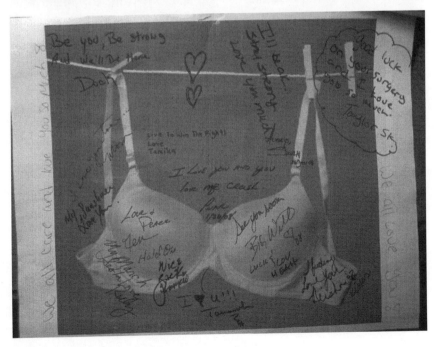

January 27, 2008 Surprise from Aunt Pat

I was sleeping hard this morning. Reality was simply a dream as I rested, not a care in the world; the sleep temporarily rescuing me from my real-life nightmare. I felt something on my nose. I brushed it away and tried to continue on with my sleep. I felt it again. Annoyed, I began to open my eyes as something pressed against my nose. I tried to adjust my heavy sleepy eyes, thinking I was seeing things. *I can see Pat's face, but she is in Georgia, isn't she? I must be asleep; dreaming.* I grabbed the face in front of me, palming her cheeks, still adjusting to the morning light and trying to hold onto one of my favorite people. I thought if I held her face close to me she'd stay. I needed her here with me. Then, I realized that it was real. Pat was here! It was my aunt; my friend; the person I look up to. I do not remember how I got out of the bed, but next thing I knew, I was on the other side of my bedroom, with her in my arms jumping up and down. We screamed, cried and cried, and screamed. She flew in to be with me for my surgery and for three days following. Pat being here means so much. She came to Philadelphia from Georgia to be with me during this difficult time. I do not know how I can express to her just how much this has lifted my spirits.

Pat bought me a beautiful wig, an inspirational journal and gifts (clothes) for my children.

January 28, 2008 Last Day at Work, Day Before Surgery

My workstation was busy today. As soon as one visitor left, another one came right in. Co-workers came to share love, prayers and encouragement. I received an abundance of flowers and cards. Aaron, Kelly and Kendra (co-workers) took me to Bertucci's for an Italian lunch (my favorite cuisine).

I went to discipleship class today. Andrea (Aunnie), my discipleship teacher, decided to change things up a bit in my honor. I needed to be with my sisters-in-Christ the day before my surgery. We sat in a circle on the floor with covers and pillows (slumber party style). We talked about life, trials, faith, trust and hope. We talked about support, friendship and love. We laughed like teenager girls at a sleepover. It was so warm, fun and uplifting.

Joey came home with about a dozen cards signed by his teachers and friends at Wissahickon Middle School. The cards wished me well, sent blessings, offered support and encouragement.

My mom, Pat, Bianka, Candice, and Shan and I went to Friday's for food (a plethora of appetizers) and cocktails so I could have a good time, to ease the tension, before the big day. I couldn't eat after midnight (or I could eat all I wanted before midnight) so we pigged out and drank until about 11:00 pm. When I got home, my nerves were so bad that I decided to have a glass (or two) of wine before midnight came in. At 11:59 pm, I took my last sip of the chilled glass of zinfandel.

I double checked my bag for the hospital stay. Clothes, *check*. Toiletries, *check*. Journal, pens, picture of kids, underclothes, night clothes, footies, chapstick, toothbrush, *check*.

January 29, 2008 – February 1, 2008
The Day of My Bi-lateral Mastectomy with Tissue Expander Insertion, Chestnut Hill Hospital

My parents, Tony and Marnita, Candice, Pat, and friends Shan and Laneishia (Neish), one of my best and dearest of friends, accompanied me to the hospital. They stayed with me until the last minute. I was asked to take a urine test as they like to be sure patients are not pregnant before going into surgery. I filled out a few consent forms and dressed into my gown. I sat on the bed waiting to be taken to the emergency room. Daddy and I had a moment of prayer. Not once did I feel any anxiety or fear. Not until I was rolled into the operating room and they began to hook me to the monitors, positioning me for surgery. I cried hysterically. The nurses tried to soothe me with a kind look, a soft smile, a stroke across my arm and shoulder and a tug on my toe. They offered something to relax me. *Yes! Give me something, quick!* Instantly, I felt like I had a couple of cocktails. Before I knew it, I was waking up… three hours later.

I lie in the recovery room with pain like none I had ever experienced. I think I would have rather been in labor again. OMG! I could not move left or right in fear of the pain shooting through my entire body. I was a little delirious, but knew I had come out of surgery. I was scared and all I wanted was my mother so I whispered to the nurse to get her for me. I felt like it hurt to even talk. My mom rushed to my side thinking something was wrong. She then realized that I just needed her. No words needed to be exchanged. I just needed her. She held my hand, stroked my face and hair and it soothed me.

Moments later, the orderly came to transport me to my room. He attempted to make small talk; paid me a compliment. Nice guy, but who can think about making casual conversation at a time like this? *I'm in pain! I don't want to talk to you! I'm not feeling pretty! Do I look fine?! Just shut up, get me to my room and pump me with drugs!*

My three-day-stay in the hospital was…eventful. Originally, they said I could go home the following day if I felt well enough. But pain shot across my chest. I could barely use my upper body because of the pain. I was not going anywhere.

I was pumped with a morphine drip, took stool softeners, Dilaudid, Percocet, and was injected in the stomach with Heparin twice a day. The Heparin was to prevent blood clots.

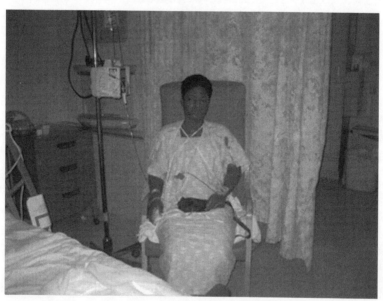

Going to the bathroom was so frustrating. I had to make sure I had my drains, morphine drip and IV secured. I could barely walk to the bathroom without getting dizzy. I could smell all of the medication in my urine. It was a struggle trying to wash my hands while holding the drains and tubes; not to mention, doing all this with the pain that seemed to shoot throughout my entire body. Most times Shan held everything so I wouldn't get tangled in the tubes or snag something. Can you imagine?

Sleeping was out of the question unless I was heavily sedated. I was awakened every couple of hours so the nurse could check my vitals. Other times, I was awakened by the pain because the medication had worn off. All night, I'm raising and lowering the bed trying to get comfortable. I could not roll over without Shan's help. She, or the nurse, would have to push me to a sitting position, reposition my pillows under and around my head, arms and feet. She would then have to help me lie down. This happened several times a night. Poor thing barely got any rest as she was up throughout the night just as often as I was.

Fortunately, I did not experience any nausea after coming out of anesthesia. I actually wanted to eat just hours after being taken to my room. Pat, my mom and Shan teased me with chips, snickers and juice as they passed it by my face and shoveled it into their mouths. *Just wrong! I'm starved!*

The nurse gave me the ok to eat something light as long as I felt my stomach could handle it. My dad ran out and bought me strawberry ice cream. *Yum!* I could not get it down my throat fast enough. Later that evening, I had chicken broth, pudding, jello and Ocean Spray white cranberry juice.

By day two, I was able to eat the French toast Shan bought for breakfast and the hoagie my brother Michael bought me for dinner.

Come the end of my stay, my room was beautiful. It was filled with cards and an assortment of flowers. I even received a couple baskets of fruit flowers. *Delish!*

When I was transported to my room, after surgery, I believe my first phone call was from Amy, one of the paralegals with whom I work. She called to see if I was settled in my room and to see how I was doing. It was a pleasantly surprising call. Thanks for thinking of me, Amy.

Hospital visitors were my brother Anthony, his fiancée Amanda, my brother Michael, his girlfriend Lisa, Shan, Dad (Tony), Mom (Marnita), Ellsworth, stepmother Lisa, sister Candice, Aunt Pat, Great Aunt Norma (Mopie), Aunt Bianka, Uncle Jay, Aunt Dawn, friend Sharrie, friend Sherell, Michelle (co-worker & friend), her husband and mother, friend Tamarah, and Pastor Gwen of St. Peter's Lutheran Church in Philadelphia.

I sat under Pastor Gwen's spiritual guidance for most of my childhood. I just loved her warm heart, big smile and the feeling of understanding, compassion, sincerity and love every time I saw her. When she walked in my room, surprising me with her visit, I felt everything was going to be ok. During the time of her visit, I felt like the pain and discomfort seemed to ease. She sat and talked with me for some time asking how I was doing with all of this; offering encouragement and support. She prayed with me; leaving me feeling hopeful and less distressed.

It was frustrating because I had not seen my plastic surgeon (Dr. "Surgeon") as scheduled. Last time I saw him was before the surgery. I was told he was not well and would see me the morning of my discharge. However, Dr. Bailey came to see me, which was extremely comforting. Her staff came in at least twice a day to follow up with me.

I was discharged with two drains and a prescription for Oxycodone – APAP 5-325 (take every four hours) to help with the pain. I was instructed to get Senna (stool softener) over-the-counter since the pain medications tend to cause constipation.

The nursing staff was great. I want to remember and give a special thanks to the nurses who provided me with superb care, and who were extremely attentive, pleasant, informative, comforting and simply had all-around wonderful bedside manner: Chestnut Hill's Albert, Darlene, Joanne, Abby and Jessica.

February 1, 2008 Home Sweet Home

Shan and I managed to get home in the pouring rain. Shan brought in all of the gifts I received in the hospital. It made my bedroom smell so beautiful. It was welcoming. Flowers and cards filled both of the windows in my bedroom; juicy, delicious fruit flowers covered my night stand.

February 3, 2008 The Most Comfortable Gowns. Easy Drain Storage

Bianka and Duck bought me some nightgowns that button from top to bottom. These gowns came in handy for easy storage for drains. I could even pin the drains to the inside of the gown so they were not exposed. I could also rest the bulbs in the pockets of the gown so my hands were free when I needed to move about. The buttons eliminated the fight of having to pull something over my head since it hurt to use my arm and chest muscles.

Still in a great deal of pain. I can hardly move most of the time. That is, unless I have a bunch of pain meds in my system. Shan has to help me wash, get dressed, walk…it's frustrating being 100% dependent on someone when I have always been so independent. I do thank God for her and all she's doing though. It's just frustrating feeling so helpless. I really don't know how I would manage if she were not there the way she's been.

February 4, 2008 I Just Want Sleep!

It hurts to sneeze, laugh, cough and take a deep breath. I can not lie on my back or my stomach. I do not get much sleep because it is uncomfortable to lie on my side and it seems all the pillows in the world are not helping. I position and reposition myself and comfort never comes. The comfort of my queen-size pillow-top mattress does not compete with the pain and discomfort. Even the "range rover" pillow (as we call it), that wraps snug around my neck, brings little relief. I toss and turn while trying not to get tangled up in my drains. It's miserable spending every night like this.

My brother Michael, who's full of laughs, and his friend Lisa brought over some ice cream which provided a temporary distraction and pleasure until the pains overwhelmed me. Sometimes I hate that I can't hide the discomfort I am in. I can see the look of sympathy in the eyes of my visitors, wishing they could do something to take away the pain I'm in. I don't want them to be sad. I want them to be jovial and have fun just like any other time they've come to see me before my cancer diagnosis.

February 6, 2008 First Complication after Surgery

I have had chills, hot flashes and a 101.4 fever for the last two days. I washed up to get ready to see Dr. "Surgeon" today when I felt liquid pouring down the right side of my body. I looked down and my breast was leaking blood and fluid. I had to let Shan bandage me up well enough to get me to the hospital. Dr. "Surgeon" informed me that I had an infection in the right breast. He removed the drain then pressed and squeezed as infection poured out. He said it was best to have the expander removed. He suggested I come in the next day for removal, but said it could be done in the office. I was frustrated and insisted he remove it now to get it over with. Why did I do that? It was like being awake for a mastectomy. I left with a hole in my chest and emotionally distraught. I had no right breast.

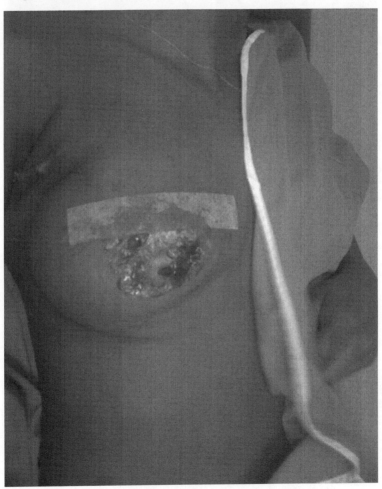

Exposed expander. Damaged skin with infection

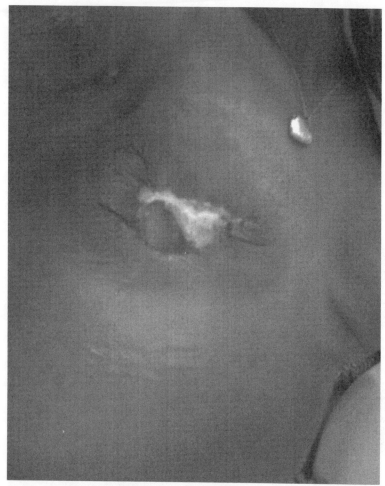

Open wound of area where expander was removed

February 8, 2008 Echogram

Before starting chemo, they needed to check the condition of my heart. The echogram was scheduled at Chestnut Hill. It was a quick and easy test. It was similar to an ultrasound. In and out. My heart is good.

February 9, 2008 Thank God for Shan

I have not looked at myself since the removal of the right expander. She has to change my bandage twice a day. I look off to the left (out the window or at the photo, on my wall, of a woman lying on the bed with her bible) in hopes of not catching even a single glimpse of what has happened to me. This has been so devastating. The whole point of leaving the hospital with the tissue expanders was to feel like I was leaving with breasts. Now this…

It takes about ten minutes to thoroughly clean and bandage the wound. It has to be cleaned inside and out with wound wash saline solution (found at any drug store) or warm soapy water. It is then packed with several squares of gauze and then covered with two ABD bandages and taped down with paper tape. Paper tape seems to be less harsh on my skin.

Candice sits on the side of me, holds my hand, wipes my tears, strokes my hair and whispers words of encouragement while Shan is cleaning my wounds and changing my bandages. Shan says my mom sat downstairs in my living room crying because she was not feeling well and could not come around me with her cold. She wanted to take care of me and couldn't be near me with my open wound. She felt helpless, but at the same time, her motherly instincts took over and she refrained from coming in my room to protect me from catching her cold as I was susceptible to infection. She sat downstairs crying, feeling her child, a part of her, was suffering and there wasn't much she could do to help.

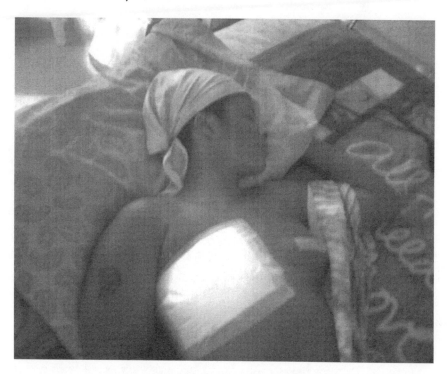

February 11, 2008 Discussing Chemotherapy
Treatments with Dr. Domchek, Pathology Report

This is my first appointment since the mastectomy and tissue expander procedure. We discussed the treatments that I will be receiving. I will be getting AC once bi-weekly for eight weeks. I will then get Taxol once bi-weekly for eight weeks.

My pathology report shows the following: I have invasive carcinoma. My tumor size is 2.5 centimeters. I am stage two (over two centimeters and node negative) and grade III. Lymphatic involvement was absent. Margins of resection are negative. My estrogen receptors are negative. Progesterone receptors are weak and HER-2 based on IHC (immunohistochemistry) is negative.

February 12, 2008 Losing Weight from Stress and Healing from Surgery

Lost a total of 16 lbs. I went into this thing weighing 148 pounds. It has been terrible since surgery. Pain keeps me struggling to breathe in deep and catch my breath.

I slipped into depression something awful. I can't/don't want to eat. Don't want to talk to anyone. Don't want anyone to see me. I cover the mirrors so I don't see myself. I just want to stay in my bed, hide from myself; hide from the world and sulk. I am angry, fearful and frustrated. I can't even see my children off to school in the mornings or check their homework at night. I've lost interest in everything. I lost all energy. I have got to find a way to get out of this funk before they want to medicate me even more.

February 16, 2008 Another Fruit Flower Arrangement

I was sitting on the couch having breakfast, forcing down my pills and watching Monk when there was a knock at the door. When Shan opened the door, there stood the Fruit Flower delivery guy holding the cutest pink hippo in a purple tutu, a purple "get well" balloon that displayed assortment of color band aids and a mouth watering fruit flower arrangement. Thanks Charles, Kelly and Salihya.

February 17, 2008 Visit from My Discipleship Sisters

As isolated as I wanted to be, the company of my friends lifted my spirits. Lisa, Chaun and Jamie came to visit. Like school girls having a sleepover, we ate pizza, talked, laughed, reminisced, joke. Before they left, we took the time out to praise God and then had prayer.

February 24, 2008 I Was Not Ready to See…

Took a hot bath hoping to relax. I asked Shan to help me into the tub and then allow me some time to myself. Thought I was ready. I sat in the water and peeled off the bandages on both sides. I stood up and faced the mirror on the wall to the right of me and stared at my body; a body under reconstruction. I collapsed back into the water and broke into tears. I cried in the tub for about 20 minutes. After composing myself, I stood up to reach over and open the mirrored cabinet so I could not see myself when I was ready to get out of the tub.

February 28, 2008 Depression, Channeling the Energy to Something Positive

I have been suffering from depression since they removed the expander - not really wanting to talk to anyone; not wanting to eat; wanting only to sulk. I lost 18 pounds. The doctors want to put me on anti-anxiety pills, anti-depressants and to see a psychologist. I am not for all of that right now. I just need to figure out a way to channel my energy. Most days Shan is forcing me out of bed and into the tub so I can get myself together. Bathing is physically exhausting. After a bath, I collapse on the bed wanting to crawl back under the covers.

So, Michael's and AC Moore, here we come. Shan drove me to the arts & crafts store where I loaded up my cart with clay pots, paint, brushes and clear gloss spray paint. I was excited about my new project as I rushed home to set up. I put on my gloves, laid out the newspaper and started painting pots for my plants' new homes. It felt so good to put that energy into something positive. It was extremely therapeutic.

February 29, 2008 More Pain and a High Fever

I have been up all night with the chills and hot flashes again with pain in my left arm, back and chest. My fever rose precipitously. It reached 101.4 degrees and then my left breast starting leaking! WTF!? Dr. "Surgeon" says it's a viral infection. More pills. Amoxicillin 500mg (one pill four times a day.) Sulfamethoxazole/TMP DS (one pill twice a day) and Silver Sulfadiozine 1% cream for breast. Ten days' worth. I am waiting to hear back from Robin to see if my chemo will be delayed yet again. I'm supposed to start March 5th.

March 4, 2008 Ignorant-Ass People (Sitting in the plastic surgeon's waiting room)

These damn women are so stupid. So clueless and insensitive. Here I am, me and another woman, here to see a plastic surgeon because we HAVE to, not because we want to. These bitches are sitting here cackling about the work they want done and how much time they wish they could spend in the gym. But since they can't spend that much time in the gym, they plan to Botox this, shoot up that, lift this, pull that. Maybe I just don't understand because I am only 29 and still considered to have my youth and have yet to deal with issues of aging. Or maybe I'm just being overly sensitive. But give me a f*ckn' break! Do they have any clue as to what it means to love yourself for who you are and what you have; what you have been blessed with? Insensitive bitches. I asked Shan to come get me when the nurse called my name and I walked out of the waiting room. I wanted to smack the hell out of them and give them a piece of my mind.

March 5, 2008 First Chemotherapy Treatment at University of Pennsylvania Hospital

Last night, Aunt Mopie cooked chicken, corn pudding, cabbage and yams. Bianka bought pizza and hot wings to add variety for the kids. We prayed, ate, laughed and watched movies. We wanted to do something before my first treatment to keep my spirits up and the anxiety down. It's non-stop laughter when my family gets together. We eat, have some wine, reflect on the past and find the humor in the present.

I packed a snack, Gatorade, a book, my journal, a movie and the quilt my mom made to take with me to my appointment.

This morning, I suffered from a bit of anxiety. I guess that is to be expected as this is all new to me. I'm scared and upset and the anger from my diagnosis is coming back. *Why me?* I felt a little tension headache coming on. The ache crept up my neck. I'm scared to take anything for it as I am minutes from having this "poison" injected into my system. Yes, this is supposed to kill cancer, but what is it doing to the rest of me? I've been told, "We make you sick to make you better." Sigh…

I can't breathe. My eyes are swelling up, but I force myself to take deep breaths and close my eyes to fight back the tears. I can't help but to look around the waiting room and wonder how many are here for the same thing. How many are feeling the exact way I am feeling at this very moment. *CAN ANYONE HEAR ME SCREAMING*!

I stared out of the window at Philadelphia's beautiful skyline and said "God, this is your will. So it shall be done." I know it's not about me, but about Him. I don't have to understand it right now. Just have to go along with His plan.

Dr. Bajor complimented me on my hair cut. I was flattered. He and Dr. Domchek did a follow-up before sending me to be prepped for chemo. Afterwards, I checked out, paid my $40.00 co-pay and headed to the treatment center. Shan and I sat quietly while I waited about ten minutes to be called to my room. Theresa took me to a private room with a reclining chair, gave me a blanket, a television and offered me a beverage. She also asked if I wanted a portable DVD so I could watch a movie for the duration of my treatment.

My IV was put in place in my left hand. I was given an anti-nausea medicine which was a fifteen minute drip. I could feel the cool sensation going up my arm though my veins. Theresa then took what looked like a large syringe and injected the Adriamycin which looked like red dye. My wrist itched as it traveled through my veins. This took just a couple of minutes. The Cytoxan was hooked up next. That was a 20 minute drip. I felt nothing right away, but I had butterflies in my stomach something awful. I was fully aware I was sitting there getting a chemotherapy treatment, but it really hadn't hit me. Surprisingly, I was fairly calm; little to no anxiety.

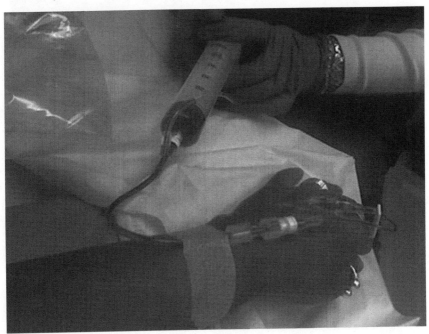

I felt fine leaving the hospital. Then, as soon as the sun hit me, I felt tired. I slept in the car on the way home while Shan drove. She parked in front of the house and let me sleep for a half hour before waking me to bring me inside. I woke, came in, told my mom about my experience and felt tired again. I went to bed at approximately 8:00 pm and slept the entire night.

It seems I've slept 70% of the day for the three days following chemo. I also experienced some queasiness so I didn't have much of an appetite. My urine was a red/orange color. I hear drinking plenty of water will help flush the chemo out of my system and reduce nausea and fatigue.

March 8, 2008 Uplifting Company

My discipleship sisters from the Church of Christian Compassion came to visit. Audrey, Arlene, Ms. Vernell, Ms. Lillian, Sunny and Quinetta all came to offer their love and support. I was still having a down day from chemo so I stayed in the bed. They cooked and brought food for the children and me to have in the house, so there would be prepared meals ready for the family. It was such a blessing. I couldn't cook if I tried because I was so tired all of the time. On the menu was lasagna, turkey wings, peach cobbler, string beans, beef soup and mac & cheese. Quinetta bought me the most comfortable pajamas and a bath & body set.

We had prayer, song, broke bread and enjoyed some laughs and cries.

March 9, 2008 Putting Weight Back On

I weigh 138 lbs. I am getting my appetite back and putting a little weight back on.

March 10, 2008 Feeling Good Again

Almost feel back to normal today. Today was a good day. No queasiness or fatigue. I managed to get out of the house. I went to Blockbuster then to the post office to take care of some business.

Something I hadn't been able to do for awhile because of the fatigue, pain and infections. It felt good to be out of the house.

March 11, 2008 Damn Neulasta

I ache all over. It felt as if I had been in a fight. My back, head, legs, arms – everything aches. Motrin is helping a little, but not much. I was irritable and got frustrated with my hair just touching me. I just started grabbing and cutting more of it off. Feel like I'm going crazy!

March 12, 2008 Pains and Fever, Again

99.4 fever. Still having pains in my back, neck and chest all on the left side. Dr. "Surgeon" says its seroma (build-up of fluid). So, it has to keep draining (run its course).

March 13, 2008 Discomfort. More Bad Expander News

I haven't slept. Have shooting pains, chills and fevers. Allyson, visiting nurse from UPenn, visited and suggested I call the doctor. Dr. "Surgeon" suggested I come in right away. Shan drove me to his office where she practically had to carry me to the building. I had to walk to his office clenched to Shan's arm because the pain shot through me and I could barely stand up straight or walk. Joey had to help me sit up and lie down this morning because I couldn't move on my own. I needed help getting to the bathroom because the pain was just that bad. Every time I moved the pains shot through my back and chest.

Dr. "Surgeon" informed me that the skin is not healing correctly around the expander so the expander is exposed. The seroma (fluid build-up) is causing the pain because the fluid is trapped and is causing pressure. There is no sign of infection. The skin is thin and not durable enough to handle the expander. So, the expander has to be removed. WHAT THE #*#*!?

March 14, 2008 Removal of the Left Expander

My mom, Uncle Jay, Shan and I got to the hospital at 10:00 am so they could start prepping me for surgery. I paid my $125.00 co-pay then headed to the next room. They drew my blood to check my white blood count, took my temperature, blood pressure and asked if I ate or took any pain medication since midnight. I had not. As a matter of fact, I didn't get any sleep either from the pain, chills and the 100.4 fever.

I was taken to the back to change. With all the pain I was in, it took me ten minutes to get my gown. I made an attempt to hold the gauze in place on my leaky breast while pulling the gown up my arms and over my shoulders. They put my wrist bands on and helped me into bed. The anesthesiologist inserted my IV and antibiotic while telling me about his 12 and 15 year old children. This was a temporary distraction as I told him about my 11 and 12 year old.

Dr. "Surgeon" stopped by to visit me while I sat up in the bed in pain. It was comforting to have him show his face before the surgery. He told me I'd be feeling better soon and that he would be able to fix all of this. I just had to be patient and get through chemotherapy.

Moments later, I was being rolled into the operating room. I told them I needed something for the pain. They injected something into my IV and next thing I knew, I was feeling like I had too many cocktails. I remember sliding over from my bed to the operating table and taking off one of two robes. I don't remember lying down or anything. The next thing I knew, I was waking up and surgery was over.

Relief! I felt like I could walk out of the hospital and do cartwheels. My mom and Shan walked into the room saying my eyes even looked brighter (indicating a jaundice-type look). It hasn't hit me or upset me that I don't have either breast now. I am just so happy to not be in the pain I was in. I have been miserable the last few days.

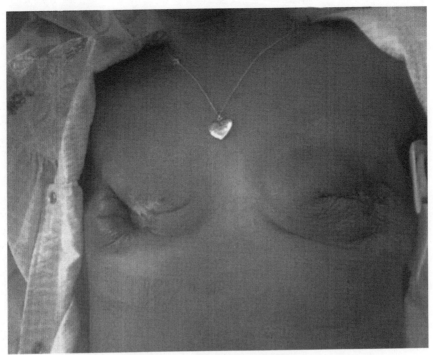

My wounds a couple of days after left expander removal

I did have a drain put in place, but I don't care right now. It should only be in for a week or so. I'll deal with it. I'm just so happy to not be in any pain.

I was hungry after leaving the hospital. We stopped at Olive Garden and had a nice lunch of soup, salad, fish and pasta. I washed it down with a peach iced tea. OMGosh! RELIEF! I can't believe how well I feel.

Sharrie came over with her clippers so Joey could cut my hair. He's been asking to cut it since learning I wanted to cut it even shorter. Sherri suggested I not be too dramatic and to just shave it short instead of bald. I decided to go with short. Joey shaved my head most of the way before he started to look as if he lost interest. At least we shared the moment. I guess it was more work than fun for him. Lol

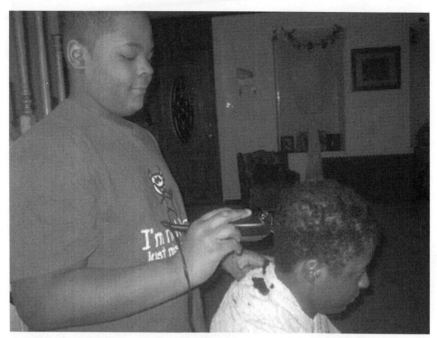

Sharrie took over and even let my mom try a section. They shaped me up and finished with cleaning up my side burns. I sat wondering what I looked like and how I would react.

I looked in the mirror after Sharrie dusted the hair off of me and wiped me down with alcohol. I don't think I look too bad. I still have to get used to it. Joey and I actually look a lot alike.

March 15, 2008 Relief!

I slept for an entire night. A whole night of sleep! Thank you Jesus! The kids and I are going to Dave and Busters!

As I prepared for my day out with my children, Dr. "Surgeon" called me himself to check in on me. I was surprised by the phone call. It was thoughtful calling me at home to check on my progress.

I look like...a boy. I look like my son. I wanted to feel I resembled some femininity. Before leaving for D&B, I stood in the mirror and put on my earrings, eyeliner, lip liner and gloss. I felt I looked as if I were a drag queen getting ready for a show. I guess I am still adjusting to this shaven head.

March 16, 2008 5:22 am Nightmares

*Stretched across the bed, positioned like a human sacrifice, I could feel the witch doctor penetrate me as I squirmed to get free. "What does this have to do with anything?" I asked myself. I rolled over and tried to crawl away when I could feel him once more. He grabbed a **syringe** and jabbed it into me. The **red dye drained from the syringe and into my blood system.** I watched as my **nails** instantly **turned black**. I leaped from the bed screaming. I asked, "What have you done to me? I made a mistake. This should not have happened," I screamed. What was I going to do? I ran into a nearby room and dialed a number. I explained to El what happened as I sat in a fetal position on the floor behind a cream colored couch. **My hair slid from my head and onto the floor**. Someone walked by and handed me a vanilla cream cookie as big as a Frisbee. Someone else walked by and stroked my shoulder as if to bring me comfort. I jerked away as I read a number (call waiting) that appeared on the phone and was listed as The Shop. I told El what the number said. He said, "Sounds like a place from back home." He told me I should apologize to the "doctor" and allow him to finish. I asked if he was sure and he assured me this was how things had to go. Was this all supposed to make me better? I hung up, found the "doctor", hugged him and told him I was sorry and trusted he was able to heal me. He looked up at me with a grin, nodded his head in acceptance of my apology and then… I woke up.*

WTH! THIS STUFF IS GIVING ME NIGHTMARES!

March 18, 2008 My Hair is Starting to Fall Out

I noticed more hair in my underwear. I am starting to notice strands shedding from my head. I've been struggling with having had both expanders removed. I'm starting to feel I've had a major setback. Dr. "Surgeon" assures me this is unfortunate and it does happen, but he can fix it and I will be pleased.

March 19, 2008 Second Treatment

I sucked on a messy Popsicle while they administered the AC. Megan, the nurse, said people claim it helps them with discomfort from mouth sores.

Megan, sweet girl, but she acted as if I were the first person she had put a damn IV in. She tapped my vein for about 10 minutes looking for a vein. As if my nerves weren't bad enough, I look down and she had blood everywhere. I wanted to smack the crap out of her and ask for another nurse. Before I could part my lips to say "Get someone else," Theresa walked in and took over.

Everyone was very accommodating. They made sure I was comfortable in the lounge chair which was seated by a large window overlooking the city. I was given a blanket to keep warm and the remote to the television to stay entertained. I watched *I am Sam*. Shan bought Chinese so we pigged out on roast pork lo mein and pepper steak & rice. It helps to eat what you enjoy.

I left with that "sinus headache" feeling from the Cytoxan and went home to rest it off.

Other than the metal-like taste in my mouth, I feel okay. Some foods taste bland. I no longer enjoy my favorite apple martinis. They taste different. Wine still tastes the same though.

I have to go back to the hospital at 12:30 pm tomorrow to get the dreaded Neulasta shot.

March 20, 2008 Neulasta Shot, Medical Bill, Bandages

My mom, Shan and I drove downtown for the Neulasta shot. I got it in the back of my arm again. I was told the shot in the stomach was not so bad, but after those Heperin shots, during my hospital stay after the mastectomy, just has me a little skeptical. Those were painful.

If I am reading this correctly, the bill for my bi-lateral mastectomy with tissue expander insertion came to $80,499.80. Thank God for health insurance. My balance (responsibility) came to $750.00. How do they expect you to cover these payments? I'm only getting 60% of my income while on medical leave. That's pretty much nothing to cover all of my expenses as it is. It seems timing has worked in my favor from the start though. The way my last check from work fell into place, bills got paid and income tax followed shortly after. I can not complain too much. I have been blessed. This bill will get paid. I'm leaving it in God's hands. I have enough to worry about (that I should also be putting in God's hands).

The tape is starting to make my skin raw. I am in pain with every change of my bandages. So I decided to try something different. Shan cleans and packs my wounds as usual, but instead of tape, I hold the ABD bandage in place while Shan wraps an ace bandage around me. It holds the bandages and drain in place. This saves me from the pain from the tape making my skin raw and peeling it off with each change. Only thing, it gets itchy, but I'd rather the itch than the tape tearing at my skin.

March 21, 2008 Left Drain Removed, Magic Mouthwash & Ulcer Ease Prescribed

Robin at UPenn called in a prescription for magic mouth wash and ulcer ease. They are to help with the mouth sores. They taste horrible, but I hear they help a great deal.

The drain was removed today. I still have to go back to have the stitches removed. I took some Oxycodone, before I met with Dr. "Surgeon", to prevent any pain. It helps. I don't know if it's the chemo or the Oxycodone, but I have been sleeping on and off all day. Fatigue is kicking in. So, I allow myself to drift off into my cat naps. Shan bought me a twin size air mattress so I am able to rest and relax in the living room comfortably. It gets depressing lying in the bed all day away from everyone. So I have the comfort of a bed while spending time in the living room watching movies, laughing and such with the family and friends that stop by.

March 22, 2008 Celebrating My 30th Birthday

Since cancer interfered with my trip to Italy with my sister (a surprise gift from her), we (Candice, Bianka, Shan and I) went to Bistro Romano for a theater dinner to celebrate. It was set up as if we were on a cruise and had to solve a murder mystery. It was fun, entertaining and the food and service was great. After putting our heads together we figured out who the killer was, but another table was picked and they won the $50.00 gift certificate to dine at the restaurant. We had a really nice time. Candice and I rescheduled Italy for March 2009.

March 23, 2008 Easter

It's Easter and I can't move from off of the air mattress. God bless Sharrie for coming over and making lamb chops, green beans and pasta for dinner. I managed to make a basket for the kids, but was later confined to the mattress when the pains started in my chest and back. My temperature rose and the chills kicked in. *This can't be happening!*

March 24, 2008 My 30th Birthday

I lie there, Shan and Allyson (the visiting nurse) standing over me trying to take my vitals. I could barely move as the pain was so intense. Shan said I lie there lethargic, staring out the window and into the sky. She said she called out to me and I looked in her direction, not at her, but through her. She said it was the first time it hit her that I was *really* battling cancer; I was really *sick*. She said it scared her as I looked as if I were dying. She and Allyson decided it was time for them to get me to the hospital and they needed to get me there quickly.

I arrived at the University of Penn Breast Cancer Clinic with pains in the right side of my chest and back and a 101.7 fever. Dr. Finlay, Robin and Theresa put in the IV, gave me a dose of morphine, which did absolutely nothing, and drew some blood to begin taking tests. They also did a culture on the site where my drain was located.

The pain hadn't subsided after my dose of morphine. I needed and wanted to be anesthetized right away in hopes getting relief from the pain and anguish. I was given 5mg of Dilaudid which helped almost immediately. I was moved, temporarily, to another floor since the clinic was closing and my hospital room was not ready. I was taken to a private room. I was given antibiotics intravenously which was an hour and a half long infusion.

Ms. Phillips (Shan's mom) and Ms. Dianne (her friend) sat with me while Shan saw to it that I got registered for admission. While we waited, three nurses (Eileen, Terry and Clarice) from the 15th floor Cancer Chemotherapy Unit, walked in singing Happy Birthday with three donuts and candles on a plate. It lifted my spirits because I was so depressed about spending a milestone in the hospital when I was supposed to be wine tasting and taking a cooking class in Tuscany. *At least I'm alive, I guess.*

I was taken to admissions where I met Monique who helped me finish up my paperwork. She was fairly new on the job, but gave me the impression that she had been doing that for some time and made the transition so smooth. She wished me happy birthday, as everyone had been doing, and saw me to my room.

I was admitted to room 7020 in the Rhoads building. I was craving French fries so Shan went to McDonald's to get us some dinner. The nurses: Sara and Emmy and Dr. Vorwich came in to check my vitals. Heart rate high (110), Blood Pressure good (109/76), Temperature high, but steady (101.7).

At about midnight, after being laid up in the bed, poked, probed, injected, squeezed, etc., I got restless and decided to walk the floor. I discovered the family room had a television, games, and a computer. I was ecstatic. I was able to reply to some of my emails and get some homework done on discussion board. I was getting worried because it was nearing the deadline for some of my assignments. Plus, this would make my hospital stay less distressing.

March 25, 2008 Things Just Seem to Keep Getting Worse

I didn't sleep much. Fever is down to 99.9 this morning. Shot up to 102.2 last night. I was bombarded with a team of surgeons who rambled on about wanting to cut into me and drain the infection. They examined my left side which was so swollen it could have been mistaken for an actual breast. I was wheeled downstairs to have an ultrasound so they could get a clearer picture of the infected area.

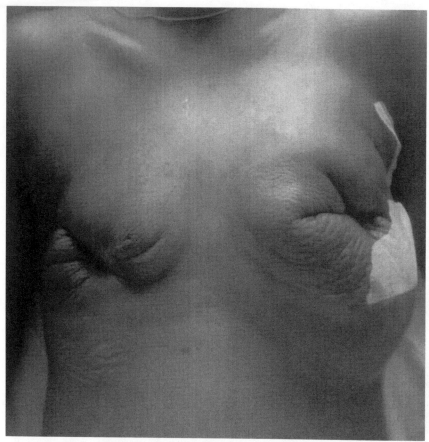

A culture was done on the wound of my left side. I tested positive for MRSA, so they are giving me Bactrim to kill the infection. I have to wear a special gown, gloves and a mask when I leave my room to protect others. Visitors have to wear a gown, gloves and mask to protect me.

My visitors today: Dad, Charles (Foy), Will, Dell, Tamarah, Robin, Dr. Finlay

My family brought my mail from the house and I had a gift from my friend Adriane who I met on Young Survivors Coalition website. For my birthday, she sent me a sweet card, a beautiful journal and a wind chime; its sound is so tranquil and therapeutic. Thanks, Adriane, for being such an inspiration. You are always in my prayers.

March 26, 2008 More Surgery: UPenn

Visitors today: Tamarah, Chaun.

This morning my temp was 101.1. I was in so much pain. I am taking a dose of pain meds every two hours. William from transport took me to radiology. I was awake for the surgery. The only thing that kept me from freaking out was the pain meds and the sheet that blocked my view of my left side. I don't know how long I was down there, but I dozed off after awhile. When I woke up in the recovery room, I felt so much relief. Temperature is down to 99.5. I am finally able to rest comfortably.

Back at my room, I was visited by the *Musicians on Call*. It was a nice visit. One woman played a guitar while the other sang *Gonna Build a Mountain*.

March 27, 2008 Visits, Kids Freak Out, How Strong Are These Meds

Debbie, Aaron, Jamie, Taylor, Joey, Kathleen, Anthony, Amanda, Audrey and Kelly came to see me today. As I laughed and joked with loved ones, the visits took my mind off of this calamity.

The surgeon came in to check in with me. Said she thought she could drain more infection from the area. She made a small incision while I lay right there on the bed. She inserted a "wick" to keep the site open and allow the area to keep draining. *I just can't take any more!*

Shan brought the children to the hospital so they could see me. She said they told her they thought I was in the hospital dying. I really need to talk more with my children about what is going on with me. I need to communicate with them about everything in hopes of them better understanding and coping.

I couldn't stop hugging and kissing my babies. Felt like it has been forever since I'd seen them. I lit up when they walked into the room. As my baby girl held tight to my hand, and my little man lovingly stroked my back, I was reminded of what was truly important and what I need to focus on as I went through this. I remembered, they are the main reasons I'm fighting.

Joey touched my hair and a clump came out. It completely freaked him out as he jerked his arm away and shook the hair free from his hand. My daughter stood there; eyes wide with fear/shock/unsettlement. I guess they did not realize how easily my hair would be falling out, even after showing them the large amount of hair that lay on the pillow.

I decided I couldn't take my hair falling out all over the place. Especially after seeing how Taylor and Joey reacted. It is shedding profusely. I let water run over my head and the sink filled with hair. I dried my head and there was just as much hair in the towel. My head is full of patches now.

I Wanna Draw Shan (in a sing-song voice)

Knowing darn well I can't draw; nodding off with each stroke of the pen, I was determined to do a sketch of Shan. All of those medications had me delirious.

Shan reflects back on that night: "I still remember that night you wanted to 'draw Shan'. You kept giggling - so proud of what you drew. Your face was so serious, as if you were making sure of every detail. I couldn't wait to see how you'd draw me - as your head kept dropping from all the heaviness of the meds. After a full 10 minutes, all you showed me was a darn stick figure! We laughed till you passed out on the food tray. You were so happy then - feeling no pain. And you slept well."

March 28, 2008 Looking Like a Cancer Patient, Mike Reminds me of our Conversation Last night

Candice, Quinetta and Meah came to see me today. I had some good laughs with my crazy sister and friend Meah. Quinetta's visit was so warm and inspiring. I am moved every time I speak to her.

Although I knew losing my hair was bound to happen, experiencing it is still troublesome; difficult. Now I **look** like a cancer patient.

Mike, my baby bro, called this morning asking how I was doing. I told him I slept hard last night from all of the meds. He asked me a question about the conversation we had the night before. I said, "Huh?" He said, "Are you serious?! We had a long lil bro to big sis talk. I poured my heart out to you! You don't remember?" Sadly, I didn't. I was so out of it. I don't know why Shan let me get on the phone. I was delirious. She said I even called my mom wanting to hear her voice and see how she was doing. Shan said I was emotional and sentimental after all the meds; I wanted to call everybody. I don't remember any of that. LOL

April 1, 2008 I Want To Give Up!

I am tired of the medication. I take pills for nausea, anxiety, pain, insomnia (I am having trouble falling and staying asleep), allergies, multi-vitamins, iron (I'm anemic), calcium (I was told it is important for cancer patients getting chemo), stool softeners (the pain medication can cause constipation), and medication to take before and after chemo treatments.

I can't do this! I can't continue with this fight. I fear the next treatment, future surgeries (reconstruction) and more complications. I am tired of the fevers and pains. I'd rather enjoy the rest of my life here on Earth, however long that time would be, than to deal with the struggles of battling cancer.

Shan took me to Applebee's to have lunch in hopes of lifting my spirits. I sat at the table. My eyes blurred and burned as they filled with tears. I put my head down and said, "I give up." Shan grabs my wallet and slides the pictures of my children in front of me. I looked long and hard at my babies and I was taken back to all of those thoughts, feelings and reminders from when I was in the hospital. I said a prayer for strength and did my best to push all of those thoughts of giving up behind me. The whirlwind of emotions is exhausting - going from anger, to fear; from victory to defeat; from hope to discouragement.

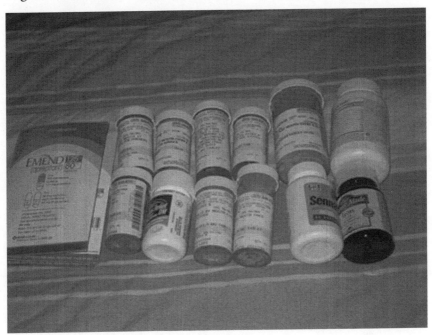

April 3, 2008 Fearing Death

This is the first time I feared death. Not so much as death as in being dead, but just no longer existing on earth or dying in pain. The fear of not being here with my children and other loved ones. Today, I realized I am battling a disease a lot of people die from. That terrifies me. Cancer; death by cancer scares me.

I have been experiencing a lot of queasiness these last few days. I am not sure if it's from the chemo, the Dilaudid (pain med) or just nerves. Today is the first time I vomited. I feel weak.

April 8, 2008 Social Worker

"Surgeon" says the infection is clearing up beautifully, but because I am getting chemo tomorrow he wants to put me on another ten days of Bactrim (antibiotics). Sigh! I hate those big-ass pills!

Met with Amanda (social worker). We discussed different financial assistance programs out there that may assist me while I am on medical leave. We also discussed having the children come in for counseling. I am concerned they may not be expressing their feelings or concerns about their mother battling cancer. I don't expect them to fully understand, as some adults don't fully understand unless it is something they've experienced themselves. God forbid.

I am learning that if I look well, people don't understand that I truly am not doing/feeling well. They don't see the night sweats, the vomiting, the pain, the lack of sleep, the irritability, the sadness, the fear. I put on my "superwoman mask" when I have visitors so they see the old Tyesha, not realizing how different Tyesha is now. Not realizing that I have moments of weakness, lack of faith, confidence and low self-esteem during this battle. I am not just affected physically, but spiritually, psychologically, and emotionally.

April 9, 2008 Third Treatment

Domchek wants me to call if the vomiting continues. I've vomited almost every day over the last week. She says I may need to come in to get hydrated. She put me on Amend, yet another pill for nausea. She also suggested I try the Celexa (anti-anxiety) to help me with my mood and appetite (I lost another two pounds. Down to 131 pounds).

Damn AC. I was fine until it was time to pump me with that red poison. It was as if I could feel it traveling through my veins. It itched, it turned my stomach, and my head began to tingle. I know all of this may be mental, but this stuff is so strong. What else is it doing to my body? I cannot help but to ask myself this question.

I am no longer wrapping in ace bandages, ABD pads or tape. It's extremely comfortable to be free of having my skin taped or tied down.

Loving my nephew, Gabriel

April 15, 2008 Scarves

First time I wore a "sister" scarf. My mom taught me how to wrap it. I don't think I'll ever where a wig again, unless I have to. The scarf is extremely comfortable and stylish. It's not hot and weighed down like a wig. A wig tends to feel like I have a darn hat on all day. It's getting too hot for those things.

April 16, 2008 Ocean City, MD

I woke up to the sun shining bright and warm on my face. I got up and stepped out onto the patio of Bruce's condo in Ocean City, MD. I glanced over the sand that had been untouched, and crashing waves as the sun kissed my skin. At 7:30 am, it is warm ten stories high. It's much cooler at ground level.

This is the first morning in a while that I didn't wake up feeling sick, feeling like I am battling cancer. This is the first morning in a while that I wanted to get out of bed and get some school work done without it feeling like such an exhausting and dreaded task. The house began to smell of sickness and medication to me. I was slipping into depression and the family knew I needed a change of scenery. I felt bordered by my infirmity.

Candice and Shan decided it was time for me to get out of the house. Candice will be watching the kids for the rest of the week. Then she will take them to my dad's place on Friday. Bruce was kind enough to let Shan and me use his place for a respite. It's a nice change of scenery.

We walked the beach, took pictures, went for dinner and drinks; spent the morning on the balcony overlooking the ocean, praising God, thanking God and asking God for mercy. This stay has been refreshing.

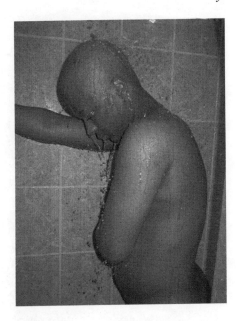

April 23, 2008 Last Dose of AC

The finger prick for the lab work is painful. It's like jabbing a sewing needle in your finger. Then they squeeze the finger to fill the tube for the blood sample.

Robin and Dr. Domchek asked if they could nominate me for a program called "Crossing the Finish Line". They say they realize this has been a rough road for me and wanted me to get a break from everything that comes with a cancer diagnosis. This organization awards trips for patients and their families. I was so pleased that they would even consider nominating me.

I got a bit emotional today while getting a treatment. I kept my eyes closed the entire time the medication was being administered. The sight of anything related to the treatment made me sick. My stomach turned at the thought of that poison going through my veins. My red blood count is low so I had to get an Aranesp shot. It stung terribly.

I asked Robin how I am to know that this is working. She says the tumors have been removed and this is like an insurance policy. She said no test will need to be run. They basically go off of symptoms from that point on. I will still need to stay on top of other scans, especially since I am BRCA1 positive.

I like Robin, Dr. Domchek's assistant. She's very informative and seems passionate about her work. She has a bubbly personality that just draws you to her.

April 24, 2008 Menstrual Cycle

Still getting a menstrual cycle accompanied by hot flashes.

April 25, 2008 AC Side Effects, Financial Award

I felt fine, but was hit with a bit of fatigue in the afternoon. I noticed discoloration on my nails, dark blotches and dry skin on my feet and spots (mouth sores) on my tongue. They say all of that is temporary.

The American Cancer Society granted me a check for personal needs. I should have the check in a week or two. The grant will go toward a credit at Rite Aid so when I get my prescriptions there will be no co-pay for the next few cancer-related prescriptions or refills. God is good! Partial credit will go towards my prosthetics. I plan to go to the Profile Shop or the Faith and Hope Boutique at UPenn for a few things.

I did not get the grant from the Patient Access Network. They only provide assistance for people who need help paying for their chemotherapy fees. Thank God mine are covered by my insurance. However, I am still waiting to hear back from Living Beyond Breast Cancer. Amanda, the Chestnut Hill Cancer Center social worker, helped me apply for the Cis B. Golder Quality of Life grant. I was told I should hear something in about a week.

May 1, 2008 Finances

I have not received a disability check in two weeks. They claim they need more medical record information from my doctors. Everyone says their forms have been turned in. I don't need this! These are some of the concerns that come with battling cancer. Not having your full income coming in; not having a steady income coming in and life around you still going on. I also learned it takes 30 days to process the paperwork

for long term disability so I won't see a check until the end of May...
if that.

May 3, 2008 Surprise from the Firm

Debbie and her sister came to visit me today. She had a gift from
Denise. It was a beautiful Papyrus journal. She then handed me a big
musical Snoopy card that had signatures all over. Inside was an envelope
from those who signed wishing me a happy birthday, congratulating me
on my graduation and showering me with get well wishes. In another
envelope was money collected from everyone. I cried (so emotional) and
gave thanks to God for the blessing while hugging Deb tight. Soon as
I'm ready to toss in the towel, God makes a way showing me He's in
control and He's going to take care of my family and me.

May 6, 2008

I've noticed some irregular spotting. Not sure if this has to do
with the chemo, but if it continues I will be sure to mention it to the
doctor.

Shan got on the phone with the company handling my short term
and long term disability. Going directly to the supervisor, they told me
no worries, they will be issuing my last two short term disability checks
first thing in the morning. I should have it by Friday.

Random Thought

I hate going out in public, sometimes. People can be so rude; so
ignorant. I know it's because they don't know or they are trying to figure
out what the deal is: *She looks sick. Is she on drugs? What's wrong with
her?* People stare. There are times my spirit is much stronger and I can
force my head up high and walk with poise; self-assurance. Then there
are times when I am too weak to even bother entertaining other people
and their ignorance. *I know you can tell I don't have any hair. I know
I look sick, weak and fragile. I know I look depressed. Your staring is not
helping! It just annoys and infuriates me.* I'm even more annoyed that I
allow myself to waste the little energy I have on other's ignorance but, I

can't help it. *Stop looking at me! It makes me uncomfortable! It makes me feel worse! Stop staring!*

May 7, 2008 Missing work, Financial Blessing, First Dose of Taxol, One of Last Four Treatments

As nice as it has been to not be on a work schedule for awhile, I miss work. I miss the daily interactions with co-workers; having another purpose to start the day; having something to do. So, Shan drove me to the firm. The love! Word got around that I was in the office and my dearest folks met in my room to see me. First it felt strange being back in the office, but shortly after, I felt right at home. I missed everyone. I missed my work, my space; daily routines outside of cancer.

I tried not to stay long as to not get anyone in trouble, but as I attempted to leave, others came to see me. They asked questions about my treatments, surgeries, the kids and if I missed work. We laughed about the impact of my absence and the longing, of some, to have me back in the office.

I lost weight. I am down to 134 pounds. My nerves are a wreck about this first treatment. Candice called to wish me luck. My mom called to check in on me.

My lab work came back ok. My blood counts were good, but I am still slightly anemic.

I had to take five tablets of Dexamethasone (steroid) last night. Then another five this morning. I was given Tagement (a fifteen minute drip) to prevent my stomach from releasing antihistamines that cause nausea and Benadryl (fifteen minute drip) to prevent an allergic reaction to the Taxol. Then they do a flush so the medicine will kick in instantly. I was a little woozy, as if I had a couple of cocktails. The Benadryl made me drowsy and put me to sleep. The Taxol was attached to my IV; this is a three hour infusion.

After my infusion, I had a bad coughing spell and vomited the apple juice I had during my treatment. The nausea quickly passed and I had an appetite.

A friend gave me a significant financial blessing today. I was surprised and humbled by the blessing. He wished me a happy birthday and congratulated me on my graduation. He assured me that he was there for me and said if I needed anything not to hesitate to ask. Thank you for the blessing. That will never be forgotten. It couldn't have come at a better time. It was needed and greatly appreciated.

May 8, 2008 Blessing from the American Cancer Society

The American Cancer Society awarded me $150.00 to go towards my prosthetics. I went to the Faith and Hope Boutique and purchased three bras and two prostheses. The prostheses go into a small slit in the bra and once I put it on, I felt like I had breasts again. It looked so natural. I figured I'd get the less expensive prosthetic since it's only temporary. I only plan to wear them when I have a blouse or dress that needs filling out in the front. Other than that, I have adjusted to not having breasts. I miss having breasts, but I have grown accustomed to my temporary situation. However, I still have not braved looking into the mirror after I bathe/shower and while I am getting dressed though.

The American Cancer Society sent me the vouchers for Rite Aid. Now all my prescriptions from my oncologist are covered. God is good. When I pick up my medication, they know to deduct it from my voucher. It is nice walking in Rite Aid and getting that familiar feeling. They greet me by name, know my medication and have me set up to grab my meds and go. Thank you, Robin and Megan, for being so kind and helpful. Amanda, thank you for helping me apply for this program.

May 10, 2008 Eastern University Commencement

Graduation, finally! I managed to pull it off, while going through chemo. I sat there through the speeches with a bag hidden under my gown (in case I got sick) and a bottle of water. Wish I could have stashed come crackers because I did have a bit of nausea. It was threatening to rain so the overcast and the slight wind helped as I get exhausted and feel weak in the sun. I also wore one of my wigs. I would have really been hot if the sun were out. I snatched that thing off and threw on my scarf as soon as I got back in the car after the graduation. It was a beautiful commencement ceremony. I felt so proud when I was handed my diploma and looked up and saw family and friends cheering me on. We met back up at my place where we sparked the grill and continued the celebration.

May 14, 2008 Living Beyond Breast Cancer Grant

Today, I received the phone call saying I was approved by the Living Beyond Breast Cancer program. I chose for my Cis B. Golder Quality of Life grant to go towards my rent, oil bill, phone bill and electric bill. What a blessing. Thank you Jesus! Thank you Amanda (Chestnut Hill Cancer Social Worker) for helping me apply for this program.

May 17, 2008 Relay for Life

The Wissahickon Valley Relay for Life, located at the Wissahickon High School in Ambler, had their annual walk today. As soon as I stepped on the turf, I burst out in tears. Seeing all of those people out there, fighting for the cure, supporting survivors, thinking about my family's history and the challenges those who battle cancer will face, overwhelmed me.

Shan and I were registered to be honored as caregiver and survivor. We were given little gifts and offered a buffet dinner. Families and friends walked the track to raise money for assistance programs and research. Luminary bags were labeled and placed around the track. As I finished my dinner, I was asked if I would be willing to carry one of the leading torches in the walk. I felt so honored! It was exciting.

I had a luminary bag placed in honor of my mom, Aunt Mopie, Linda (friend of the family) and myself.

May 21, 2008 Cleaning for a Reason

I received a message from Cleaning for a Reason letting me know I was approved to receive their services. I am waiting to hear from a janitorial service to schedule when they can come out to clean the house. This is so exciting. Thanks Stefanie (social worker from UPenn) for recommending this program. It's such a blessing to have someone to come and clean. The energy, strength or the motivation to even tidy up is scarce, when all you feel you're faced with is cancer.

Treatment wasn't so bad today. I was able to sleep through it thanks to the Benadryl. As I left the hospital, a woman in the lobby grabbed my hand and told me I will be fine; just to have faith. She told me she was diagnosed with a terminal cancer and didn't have long to live, but planned to live life to its fullest while she is here. She told me to be happy and enjoy everything as God has much in store for me. We made small talk, embraced, then parted ways. We never exchanged names. I still don't know how she knew I was a survivor. I can't recall seeing her in the treatment center.

May 30, 2008 Menstrual Cycle, RLS, Energy/Strength

It's been seven days and I still have not gotten my menstrual cycle. However, I have been hot-flashing quite often. Doctors told me chemo could throw me into menopausal-like symptoms. I suppose that's what I'm experiencing. They said my menstrual cycle should return, as I am young going through this battle and cancer is my only health issue. The hot flashes often last about ten to twenty minutes. I just start peeling off my scarf and clothes or sit on the porch and let the night air cool me off. The hot flashes usually occur in the evenings. It's weird. It's like the heat builds under the skin. So really, the air brings little relief.

Thank God I have not experienced the restless leg syndrome that is said to come with the Benadryl, which is given before the Taxol. The Benadryl prevents an allergic reaction to the Taxol. I have noticed some tingling or numbing in my toes every now and again. Robin assures me that this will pass when I am finished with chemo.

I have noticed that I am not getting around as easily as I used to: getting off of the floor, climbing stairs, household chores or long periods of walking. I experience shortness of breath and weakness. My body is still healing from the inside out and I have to build my strength back up. I keep saying I am going to get back into the gym. I really need to get motivated.

June 1, 2008 Vomiting

Today is the first time in a while I've gotten sick. I am not sure what brought it on, but I felt it coming. I took an Ativan and Prochlorperazine, but they did not have enough time to take effect. I was vomiting just as I got a bag in my hand. I can always tell when I am going to vomit. I know its coming and its coming fast when I get the queasiness in my stomach and my mouth gets extremely watery. When my mouth starts to build up with saliva, I know its coming. I know it's gotten bad because everyone keeps bags with them - even the children. The bags are kept in their pockets, pocketbooks, cars, by my bed, etc.

June 7, 2008 No Sleep, Lack of Motivation

I couldn't sleep last night. I was stretched across my queen-size pillow-top mattress and still could not relax enough to drift off to sleep.

Joey spent the night out at a friend's house. Candice came home and she, Taylor and I camped out in the living room watching movies and eating all night. I fell asleep watching movies and woke up about midnight. I got up, went to my bed and fell fast asleep. I woke up again about 3:00 am and didn't fall asleep until about 5:00 am. I was up again at 7:30 am. I didn't know how to start my day so I spent most of the morning trying to motivate myself to get it together.

June 9, 2008 Heavy Spirits

My spirit is heavy. I spent the day with my mom. She fed me a veggie omelet, applesauce and a grapefruit for breakfast and made sure I took my pills. I took some meds then drifted into a nap. When I woke, we watched movies, had eggplant wraps for lunch and washed it down with a glass of white merlot. I spent the rest of the afternoon on the computer.

June 10, 2008

I woke early to see my children off for a three day 6th grade camping trip in the Poconos. I came home and busied myself with laundry until I could no longer be in the house alone. I went to my mom's and she made me cream of mushroom chicken so I could take my meds. She gave me a pill which helped relax my nerves and I drifted off to sleep.

June 13, 2008 Getting Out with the Kids

It's going on 3:00 pm. I still don't have much of an appetite. I took this morning's medication with a cup of coffee. I believe it's just nerves. I have so many emotional things going on in my life right now. I decided to get out of the funk I am in and head to the YMCA to go swimming. It felt good to get out and enjoy the company of my children. I missed them over the last couple of days and figured a little family fun would do us (me) some good.

We swam, taught one another tricks in the water and played volleyball. I spent about 15 minutes of alone time in the Jacuzzi giving God thanks and praise for all the blessings. I thanked him for blessing us with a gym membership and for allowing me to create another memory with my children. It's moments like this, when I am down, I remember to call on God; not to ask for anything, but to thank Him for everything.

I changed from my swim cap to my scarf while still in the pool area. I wondered if the kids were embarrassed about my head as I noticed the life guard looking at my exposed scalp. My daughter said she was embarrassed because I didn't have any hair. My six year old cousin, Cameron and my son Joseph said they were not embarrassed. I guess I didn't care, at the moment. I suppose, when you reach a certain point or have been through a life altering experience, you really don't care much about what others think. I took my time and wrapped my scarf around my head, pulled out my journal and began to write as the children continued to play.

June 18, 2008 Last Treatment

Today, I had my last chemo treatment. My mother accompanied me to my appointment. It was comforting to have her there.

I was presented with a certificate of completion from the staff at the treatment center. They showered me with hugs and well wishes as they congratulated me on my making it through chemotherapy. They said they'd miss me and I promised to visit soon. They have been so good to me during this rough time. They were always so pleasant, accommodating, comforting and concerned.

Crossing the Finish Line called today. They informed me that Dr. Domchek and Robin nominated me for a trip and they wanted to get more information so they can begin looking into sending the children and me away for approximately 3-7 days.

My weight is still down. I weighed in at 134 pounds today. Dr. Domchek informed me that my weight should start picking up now that I am done with chemotherapy. She gave me a prescription for Tamoxifen. I am to start that in a couple of weeks. This is a hormone treatment to help prevent, or lower the chances, of cancer recurring. Instructions are for me to take one pill a day for the next five years. I hate the idea of being on this medication. I am now 30 years old and am not sure if I am done with child bearing. This medication will take me to my 35 year mark where risks become a factor in pregnancy. Doctors recommend you not become pregnant while on this medication because it is a possible cause for birth defects.

I told Dr. Domchek that I didn't feel the Celexa was helping much. It's supposed to help with anxiety and nausea. I plan to wean myself off once I near the end of my perscription. I feel I have been dependent on medication to get me through the days. Sleep aids get me through the night. I hate that feeling.

They took blood from my mom and me today for a genetic study to research the cause of the BRCA gene.

I noticed the dark marks on my nails from the AC are starting to fade. Now there are white lines going across my nails and they are weak and brittle. I was told that happens from the Taxol.

Candice and Joey noticed my hair is starting to grow back. I didn't really notice until I looked closely in the mirror at my scalp. My head was full of "peach fuzz". My hair is growing!

June 30, 2008 Meeting with another Plastic Surgeon (Dr. Wu) to Discuss Reconstruction, Second Opinion

Accompanied by my mom, I met with Dr. Wu to discuss my options for reconstruction. She is beautiful. She speaks with confidence and demonstrates passion for her line of work and dedication to her patients.

In my mind, I went back and forth trying to figure out if I even wanted to go through with the surgery. I had a bi-lateral mastectomy and four months of chemotherapy. I just want to put cancer behind me, especially after the complication I had while seeing Dr. "Surgeon". However, for vanity reasons, I want breasts. I want that one thing (one of the things) that makes a woman feel like a woman. Then I thought about how they won't be the same; wont get the same sensation, that natural breasts get. I will no longer experience that. I will no longer experience the feeling, the erogenous sensation that a breast/nipple does.

Dr. Wu examined me and said I was healing nicely after the debacle with the setbacks (infections and hospitalizations). I was given three options for reconstruction. 1) Tissue and muscle could be taken from my stomach (tram flap), but I do not have enough fatty tissue. Not only did I have insufficient stomach fat to use, but I heard the tram flap affects (reduces or ceases) the sensitivity to sexual stimulation. Not sure how true or common that is, but I was skeptical about the possible effects from the tram flap. So option one was out. 2) Muscle (latissimus muscle) could be taken from my back (lat flap). This procedure would take a couple hours; require a two day stay in the hospital and a four week recovery period. I was informed that it will leave a scar on my back and I would feel some weakness when lifting above the head since those muscles will be removed. 3) They could use my buttocks. However, they can only do one at a time and each time takes a six week recovery period. Bad enough my breasts were taken from me. I can accept that, now. My breasts were no good to me, but they are not touching my ass so that leaves me with option two.

So, with option two my issue is the scars because I tend to keloid. I am also apprehensive because I don't know how much my strength will be affected with those muscles removed. But as of now, surgery is scheduled for August 22nd.

August 1, 2008 Catching Up

It's been awhile since I've done some journaling. No real reason why. Not like I haven't had anything to write about. So I figured I'd take a break from homework (I'm working on another degree) and get my journal caught up. I'll begin with two funny short stories.

Short Story #1

A few days ago, I ran to the front door to grab the mail. My mailman looked at me, headed down the steps then turned back as if doing a double take. I wondered why he looked at me so strangely. Then it hit me, some time later, that I ran to the porch with a face mask on and no scarf (head still looks very bald from a distance). I was so embarrassed when I thought about how I must have looked and what might have been going through his mind.

Short Story #2

Another blooper was with this little boy, about 8 years old, who lives a couple houses down from me. Aside from the mailman incident, I'm always certain to have on my scarf any time I go outside. The day before this incident, I was on the porch and the same kid saw me…with my scarf on. The following day, my daughter, nephew and cousin played on the porch. I was on the phone with my sister describing what her son was doing. I ran outside to let him say hello to her. The neighbor was riding by on his scooter when he looked up at me, his eyes grew wide and he and his scooter hit the ground. Then it dawned on me. I was outside without my scarf. The shock of my bald head threw him off and sent him and his scooter crashing to the ground. He sat there and continued to stare. Assuring I saw no blood, indicating injury, I hid my embarrassment with laughter and I went running back into the house.

Keeping my Spirits up

I have been dealing with a lot of emotional issues lately. My baby brother has come over to visit quite frequently to get me out of the house, or to just stay in, watch movies and order out for food. We laugh, talk; he lets me vent, cry and he comforts me when I am at my worst. The company is nice. I always enjoy times with my siblings. It lifts my spirits.

My mom dragged me to the Ogontz Jazz Festival to get me out of the house and into the sun. It was nice getting out since all I've wanted to do was isolate myself from the world. After awhile, the sun became exhausting, but after a few minutes in the shade and a cold bottle of water, I was able to do a little more sightseeing. Tamarah was there helping with the production of the shows so it was fun running into her; playing throughout the day.

I recall when Debbie, Kelly, Aaron and Charles came to visit. We sat there shoveling fast food down our throats and watching Family Guy. I remember seeing that show at one time and skipped to another channel. Debbie, excited that it was a Family Guy marathon, suggested we watch it as it was one of her favorite shows. So we did. It was pretty damn funny. Between Family Guy and Married with Children, I have been able to escape my reality and laugh at these dysfunctional families.

Concerns about Job Security

One of the things that worried me was the security of my position at the firm. When my reconstruction was scheduled for the end of August with a four week recovery period, I just knew my position would be in jeopardy.

I emailed one of the partners I work for, expressed my concerns and asked his opinion. He called back and informed me that my position was secure and the firm was supportive of what I was going through and wanted me healthy and back to work when this was behind me. Shortly after, I received an email from HR responding to the letter that my doctor's office faxed to them regarding my expectant return to work date. HR stated that the firm wishes me well on my surgery and looks forward to my return to work in September. HR mentioned that if I needed anything not to hesitate to ask. I was relieved by HR and the partner's response confirming my job security.

Disability

Being on disability is a pain in the ass. Aside from getting only 60% of my income, it's been one big frustrating waiting game.

The short term disability was not bad. It did take awhile for the first check to come, but then I knew one would be in the mail every other Saturday thereafter. I was sure to put in for disability as soon as I had the date for my surgery so that things would fall into place financially.

However, when the second to last short term disability check came, there was a request for more information from my doctors before they could issue the last check and begin processing my long term disability. Then, there was a 30-day processing period before the first long term disability check could be issued. The long term disability checks come once a month. So as far as disability was concerned, there wasn't any income coming in for long periods of time. I understand completely how people could lose their homes, go into debt or ruin their credit when stricken with a life threatening disease.

Financial Blessings

I just thank God for always making a way. Reflecting back to other financial blessings: Sherell made a surprise visit and left me with a financial blessing. I was blessed with a check from a friend and a check from the Linda Creed Foundation. My stimulus check came. The American Cancer Society awarded me with a monetary blessing for prescriptions and prosthetics. Living Beyond Breast Cancer awarded me with the Cis B. Golder Quality of Life grant. The Breathing Room Foundation awarded me with a BP gas card and a gift card to Old Navy. I took the kids summer shopping. My credit card company was a blessing as well. I am enrolled in the credit protector program that guarantees a moratorium in the event of job loss, disability, etc.

Crossing the Finish Line, Update

Crossing the Finish Line awarded me, the kids and my caregiver with a seven day vacation in Ventnor NJ. We get a four bedroom, 2 ½ bath beach house with a private in-ground pool, grill and a load of other amenities. I was also given a check for spending money. We leave Monday, August 11 and return August 18. We are extremely excited!

Do People Really Understand?

Know what I realized while going through this trying time in my life? People can sympathize with you, they can care for you, let you vent, cry and scream, but they really don't understand or realize the depth of the battle.

I was having a discussion with someone about my coming to the end of my chemo treatments. We were reflecting back on all I've been through. A comment was made, I can't remember exactly what was said, but it made light of my experience. When I described what it was like, my mental and physical state, their eyes grew wide in disbelief. Although they visited often, they said they still had no idea that what I was experiencing was to that extent.

Shan used to fuss at me about my habit of not allowing people to see the vulnerable side of me. She asked me to stop dressing myself up, putting on make up and pasting on a smile when people came to visit. She always said to allow others to see the real me during this time because people didn't, and wouldn't, understand what I was experiencing.

I did my best to fix myself up and smile to hide the pain and depression when people would visit. Shan would tease me saying, "When you have visitors, you're laughing, smiling, joking, but as soon as they leave you're crying saying, 'Shan, grab a bag ('cause I had to vomit), Shan, I'm in pain, Shan, I'm dizzy, I'm weak.'" She mentioned that no one saw what it was truly like for me. No one saw me at night, tossing and turning, getting only a couple hours of sleep because of extreme pain, nausea, vomiting, depression and anxiety. No one saw me being helped to the bathroom because I was weak or in pain. No one saw me in tears as I screamed that I wanted to give up.

It is important to communicate to your loved ones (friends, co-workers, family) about what you're experiencing mentally, physically, spiritually and emotionally. Allow them to see you in a vulnerable state. Otherwise people will not understand your moods or needs. They will not know how to help you. I also realized I need not be ashamed of what I was feeling, thinking or how I looked.

Signs of Chemotherapy Fading

I noticed the dark blotches on my hands and feet are clearing up. The black marks and white lines in my nails are fading (or growing out). My energy level is finally rising again and the nausea has ceased.

The tingling in my toes has ceased. I didn't realize it until I thought about it. I haven't experienced the coldness and tingling in my toes for some time now.

Medication

Some time ago, I began to wean myself off of all of the prescription medication. That includes the Celexa (anti-anxiety). Now, the only prescription medication I am taking is the Tamoxifen. The non-prescription meds that I am taking are the multi-vitamins, calcium and iron.

I haven't experienced any side effects from the Tamoxifen and pray I don't. Knowing I cannot have children while on this medication the next five years still bothers me.

I was discussing this with my Aunt Bianka and she said I need to accept that this was all in God's plan. She said maybe it was a great thing I had my children when I did. Having them when I did was a blessing in disguise because this Tamoxifen takes me to my 35 year old mark when pregnancy is supposed to become risky. So, if I don't get the chance to bear more children, I still have my two gifts (Taylor and Joseph) from God.

Hair

My hair is really coming in now. Everyday, I look in the mirror and it looks like more and more hair. Joey rubs it everyday. Bianka wants so badly to put a bow on it. Like the one you put on a new born baby's hair. They make me sick. Lol. Candice says she can't focus on what I am saying to her because my prickly hair is waving to her. Candice is constantly talking about me needing to wax my eyebrows because my "five o'clock shadow" is distracting her. She's so mean.

The hairs on my arms and legs are coming in. Pubic, underarm hair and eye lashes have just started to come in, slowly, but they are coming in.

I must say that I have enjoyed not having to shave or buy shampoo for the last few months. No razors or shaving cream. I'd just run the soapy rag over my scalp then stand under the shower head. It feels so good.

Sleep

I am sleeping better. For awhile, I was having some restless nights; going from the floor to the bed and back, looking for comfort. Bad dreams, discomfort, and anxiety kept me up. I would only get a couple of hours of sleep when I finally drifted off. Most nights I didn't doze off until 1:00-2:00 in the morning. I was popping sleep aids almost every night. Some nights they didn't even make me drowsy.

Menstrual Cycle

Still not getting one, but I still get hot flashes every now and again. Not as bad or as frequent as before.

Body Art

My mom invited me over to have my body painted. Her friend, Cheryl Painter, has her own body painting company, *About face-face painting*. Cheryl and her friend Margie were inspired by my mom and me (breast cancer survivors) and wanted to do something to lift our spirits and let us experience what body painting was like. The brushes felt smooth and soft. The paint was cool. It was a relaxing and stimulating experience.

Margie wanted to do a rainbow with the breast cancer ribbon. I wanted the Ying Yang symbol added and the wings just came into play as she worked.

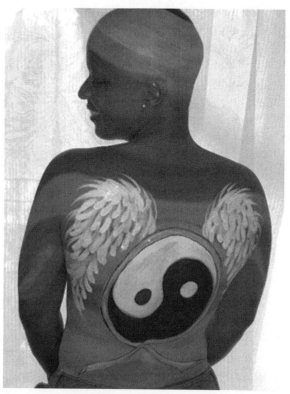

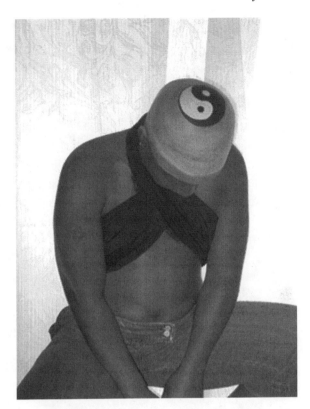

Weight/Physical Fitness

I am still losing weight. I got on the scale today and weighed in at 129 pounds. I am not happy about that. I'm thinking of getting some Insure with protein. That may help me get the weight back.

I have been going to the YMCA more often. I do a 30 minute cardio then hit the weights for about an hour. I'm trying to tone everything up. If I have to be this small, I will at least be toned.

Medical Bills

I just received a bill for $1250. It was for the week I was admitted into the hospital; the week of my 30th birthday. The bill totaled $26,849. Frustrated, I called the hospital to make payment arrangements.

My job changed our insurance from Blue Cross to Aetna in May. The co-pays for my treatments went up. But, when compared to the full price, without insurance, how much can I complain. I was looking at the full price for Tamoxifen. It's $83.00 for a month's supply, without insurance.

Night Gown with Pockets (convenient for holding the bulbs/drains)

This gown came in handy when I was in the hospital and came home because it has storage for the drains which left my hands free. Freeing my hands, it made things easier. It also kept me from accidentally dropping the bulb which would pull the drain. This happened a few times and was rather painful.

Prosthetics

Having to dress everyday and realize I had no breasts was very difficult. Seeing the shape of my body and the fit of my clothes troubled me. I was desperate for prosthetics when the American Cancer Society said they could help me get them. When they sent me the voucher for mastectomy supplies, I went to the Faith and Hope Boutique. They had bras, shirts, scarves, prosthetics, mementos, candles and so much more. Jeanette, the owner of the boutique, was very helpful. I was shown several bras. I tried on most of them, but liked three. Jeanette, Shan and I narrowed it down to the cup size prosthetics that seem to fit me best. I wore them maybe two or three times. It looked good under the clothes but...what a waste.

Now when I think back, if I could have held out, I really didn't need to waste money on them. The three bras and the prosthetics came to a little over $150. I ended up adjusting to the way my body looked. I suggest any woman who plans to have reconstruction to try loving your body, even through the changes. It's only temporary. Don't spend a bunch of money on prosthetics if you plan to have reconstruction. These things are just sitting in my drawers. I couldn't even tell you which drawer. That's how long it's been since I've bothered with them. I should have spent the money on bras for my new boobs.

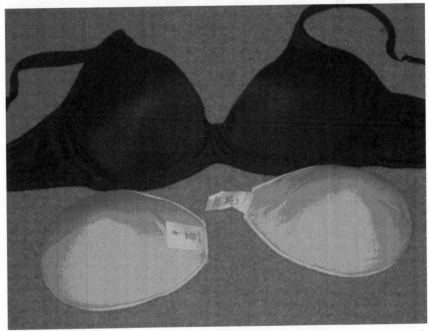

I also could have held out on the cami with prosthetics that the voucher covered. I could have used the rest of that money to go towards my prescriptions. It would have benefited me more as a credit at my pharmacy.

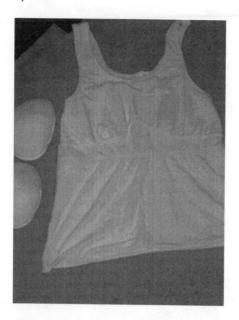

Wigs and Scarves

I haven't worn a wig since the day my mom taught me how to do the "sister scarf". The scarves are light and stylish. The wigs are so darn hot! They won't go to waste, though. I will use them when I am going through that horrible "between" stage of growing my hair back.

Cards, Phone Calls, Emails

Between Michele, Claudia, and Mark from the job, I receive cards almost every week. They constantly remind me that I am in their thoughts and prayers. The cards adorn my window panel as well as my spirits. Amy and Denise check in often via email. Debbie, Kelly, Aaron and Charles check in periodically with phone calls, text messages, emails, and visits.

August 5, 2008 Thank You!

Wrote out and mailed thank you notes to the organizations that provided me with assistance and awards. I also sent some to the nurses that cared for me.

Forgive me if I forgot anyone. I thank you all for being a blessing in my life.

Charles (Simmons) sent me a beautiful photo album with the breast cancer awareness ribbon on the cover. He also sent me a monetary blessing. Deb sent me a monetary blessing as well. Thank you both so much.

August 7, 2008 Pre-registration and Blood Work for Surgery

Today I had an appointment with Dr. Wu's nurse practitioner. I had to get blood work and sign consent forms for surgery. I arrived, checked in and sat down. I looked up and this woman sat across from me; her face scarred and swollen to the point she could barely move her mouth to talk. I looked into her eyes and burst into tears. I leaped from my seat and rushed to the other side of the waiting room. I called my mom crying. I told her what I saw and that I didn't want to go through with the surgery. She had me go to the bathroom to cry it out, wash my face and calm down. She reminded me that I still had time to make a decision.

I went back to the waiting area and the woman was on another side of the room, tissues in hand, wiping her eyes. I wanted so much to apologize to her, let her know it wasn't her. I couldn't bring myself to do it. Every time I thought to try, my eyes welled up with tears.

I was called into the room to see the nurse practitioner. She went over my current medications, allergies and asked if I had any questions. I cried the entire time.

I asked if I could see pictures of Dr. Wu's work. I saw before and after pictures. I saw pictures of the scars that are left on the backs of her patients. Dr. Wu does really nice work. It relaxed me a bit, but not completely. The thought of another surgery, healing, pain, risk for infections was disquieting.

August 9, 2008 The Love and Support of Friends

Audrey called me last night. She could hear in my voice that my spirit was a little heavy. She told me to come to her job at the Sports Club, at 10:00 am today. She scheduled me for a full body, deep tissue massage at their spa.

My masseuse was familiar with working with cancer patients. She lost her brother to cancer. During his last days, it was he who inspired her to live her dream as a masseuse. She would give him massages to relax him as he neared the end of his life.

Afterwards, Debbie took me to Texas Roadhouse for lunch. It's always great seeing Deb. She's full of comedy. The laughter helps a lot.

It has been a good day. It was great getting out and not having so much (surgery, going back to work, school, etc.) on my mind.

August 10, 2008 Another Powerful Day

It was a powerful time in church today. Today's sermon was "Everyday is a new beginning." As pastor did the benediction, he looks up at the congregation and says, "There is one more thing I am being called to do before we go down from this place."

He looks me right in the eye and asked me to come forward. I froze in place for a few seconds then warily proceeded to the front. He asked me where I was in my treatments. I told him I finished June 18th. He asked me to describe to the congregation what chemo was like. He then asked me what the next step was. I told him about the surgery coming up. He said he had no idea that something was happening so soon and knew God spoke to him, regarding me, for a reason. He looked to the congregation and complimented me on my strength and how he thanks God I don't look like what I've been through. He asked that all cancer survivors come to the front for prayer. Theresa was the first person I saw. I cried as I watched her head towards me, arms stretched out to hold me. After prayer, people wanted me to share my story. They wanted to share their story with me and some asked to exchange information with me to remain in touch to be each others inspiration and motivation. It was an amazingly uplifting experience.

My mom visited St. John's Lutheran Church in Ambler. I guess she shared my story with them. When I arrived home from church, there was a quilt laying on my bed. The label had the name and address of the church. Along side it as a poem titled *Prayer Blanket*. I was so moved by their thoughtfulness.

August 11, 2008 "Crossing the Finish Line" Respite

Made it to Ventnor, NJ in an hour and a half. Thanks to Crossing the Finish Line, we have a week respite from the stress of the last seven months.

The Stecher family offered their beautiful beach home so that I could vacation with my family. It has four bedrooms, 2 ½ baths and is complete with a private in-ground pool and gas grill. The Stecher family left a welcome note with directions to the beach, nearby restaurants, contact information and a list of things we could help ourselves to while there.

I bought them a bottle of wine and am writing notes about our experience to share with them as a thank you.

August 12, 2008 SeasIt

Todd has been wonderful these last couple of weeks. He and his wife are the founders of SeasIt, a program that offers recreation to cancer survivors and their caregivers. I was going to take a belly dancing class but could not find one in my area. I could have taken one in the city, but was not sure when I would be able to attend with surgery quickly approaching. So, I opted for bikes. Thanks Stefanie for helping me sign up for this program.

Candice called to let me know the bikes were delivered today. I am so excited about being able to go biking with my children once I am feeling well again. I have wanted a bike for a few years now. God is good.

August 18, 2008 Crossing the Finish Line Respite in Ventnor, NJ

The house was just ten minutes from the Atlantic City boardwalk and minutes from Ventnor City beach. We walked the boardwalk, relaxed on the beach, cooled off in the ocean, swam in the pool, cooked out on the grill, dined at local eateries and enjoyed a few good movies to wind down the day. It was a nice week away from everything.

My mom & kids by the pool

August 19, 2008 What a Day!

I woke up this morning suffering from a bit of anxiety. Friday seems to be coming so fast and I am full of mixed emotions about the surgery. I pulled myself together to head to my mom's house. Tyra, a photographer and close friend of the family, wanted to do a "cancer survivor" photo shoot and asked if my mom and I would be interested. We were all for it.

Tyra took shots of my mom and me together then some individual shots. We took the pictures at my mom's apartment and on the balcony. We were going to take some shots at Ft. Washington State Park, but we ran out of time.

I love Tyra's "Creative Eyes" vision and had my mom take a few shots with my camera. I enjoyed the experience. She's going to put some finishing touches on her shots and send them to us.

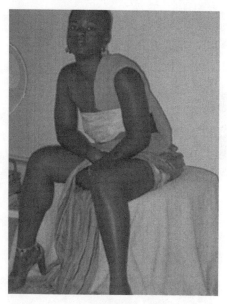

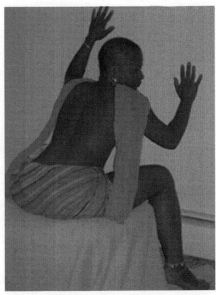

I was enjoying the experience when I got a call from the University Hospital of Pennsylvania regarding the co-pay for my upcoming procedure. I was told I would have a co-pay of $250.00 per day and I was expected to be there for two days. WHY ARE THEY TELLING ME THIS THREE DAYS BEFORE MY SURGERY!? My mood instantly shifted, my stomach started to turn and the anxiety kicked back in full force. Tyra and my mom asked what was wrong and if I wanted to stop the shoot. I was determined to finish and told them it was nothing. During the rest of the shoot, my nerves were a wreck as I tried to figure out how I would come up with the money on such short notice. My savings was depleted as I have been living off of it for the last couple of months. My disability checks just cover rent and bills so any other expenses have been coming out of my savings. I am down to almost nothing and that has to last me until I return to work and get my first check.

Debbie knew I had been suffering some anxiety and has been checking in on me. She emailed me today to ask how I was doing. I told her about the phone call regarding the co-pay. I mentioned I was ready to cancel the surgery, feeling like it was a sign that I should not get it done. I was so discouraged.

She said we'd figure something out, but I told her no worries. That was not why I mentioned it. I didn't want her worried about my issues. I just needed to blow off steam. She said that Gayle (a friend and co-worker) said she'd pay it and I could pay her back when I could. I couldn't take it from Gayle as she had just come out of (thank God) a bad health situation and has a family of her own to take care of. I told Deb that I couldn't and asked her to thank Gayle for even offering to be there for me. Deb said she understood, but was determined to figure something out.

I left the house to drop the children off at their dad's. They will stay with him until I return home from the hospital. While I sat in the car, I noticed I had two voicemails on my cell phone. I heard a message from Debbie telling me to call HR. She said that the firm was going to cover it. I called Debbie asking what she was talking about. She said, "Don't call me. Call HR." I had Deb transfer me to HR. As soon as HR heard my voice, she said, "Ty, we don't want you worrying about this. We just want you to focus on getting better and getting back to us when you can." She asked me to forward to her any bills that I received because I should not be getting them. She told me to have the hospital call her so she can give them the credit card number to cover Friday's co-pay. She told me to forward her copies of the receipts from the medical bills I have been paying because I will be reimbursed for them. All I could do was thank her and cry.

I called Debbie to thank her and she said she's not the one to get the credit. Apparently, Deb went to Kelly and Kelly went to HR.

Charles, Aaron and Kelly came to visit me. Charles bought pizza and Christian Brothers cream sherry. Charles has been planning to visit to keep my spirits up since I've been so down lately about the surgery. I kept hugging and thanking Kelly for mentioning my situation to HR. After Deb shared what was going on, Kelly said she was determined to figure something out and that's when HR told her I should not be getting the bills.

HR emailed me asking me to forward her an itemized billing statement along with payments I've already made towards some of the bills. HR said they were going to see that I get as much of my money back as they possibly could. HR said they don't want me worrying about the medical bills and insisted I focus on getting better and coming back to work when I can.

I had no idea how I was going to make this work on such short notice. God ALWAYS makes a way. The firm has been amazing throughout all of this and I can not express how grateful I am for all they have done; for all their support and encouragement.

August 21, 2008 Getting Prepared for the Procedure at UPenn

Tomorrow is another big day and my nerves are a wreck. I have been keeping busy these last few days to try to keep my mind off of it. I washed all of the clothes, took out all of the trash, did the dishes, put new sheets, pillows (Thanks Don!) and a new comforter (Thanks Daddy!) on my bed, painted my toes, dusted everything off, watered the plants and finished packing my hospital bag. I packed the night gown Bianka and Duck bought for me. It has the pockets on either side to hold my drains. Yes, I'll have drains again. The doctor said it won't be the same as when I had the mastectomy. I should only have them for about a week. I packed lotion, deodorant, underclothes, cell phone charger, medications, toothbrush and my school work. I plan to pig out on a cheese steak or hoagie and onion rings tonight since I won't be able to eat after midnight (can eat all I want before midnight).

I took the kids birthday and back-to-school shopping since I would not be able to do anything for awhile after surgery. We got everything squared away: clothes, shoes, books, hair, etc. My babies are turning 12 and 13. Sigh, they grow up so fast.

I also went food shopping so I did not have to worry about groceries or back to school lunches. Everything we need is in the house, clean and prepared so that I can simply relax and focus on recovering when I get home from the hospital.

Bianka and Duck are supposed to stay the night tonight. I know I'm in for some laughs having those two around. Candice and my mom plan to go to the hospital with me so Bianka and Duck will see to it that Gabriel, my nephew, gets to daycare. I am supposed to arrive at UPenn at 5:45 am. I'll just set my cell phone alarm for 4:00 am.

Neish called me asking what I needed and when she could come to take care of me. She's so sweet. I simply adore her. I told her not to worry too much about coming to the hospital. I told her I'll really need help when I get home. She planned to come spend a couple of days with me anyway. She wanted to cook and help me around the house.

Candice, my cousin Misty, my friend Will and I went to the movies last night for some much needed laughs. We saw Step Brothers and we were far from disappointed. It was freaking hilarious. Non-stop laughs.

Meah, Jack, Bonnie, Shani, Aaron, Debbie, Tamarah and several others called to see how I was doing with tomorrow being the big day. It's comforting hearing from my friends and knowing I have so many in my corner supporting and praying for me.

August 23, 2008 The Day after the Procedure – Getting the Expanders

The procedure was supposed to be four hours, but when I woke up, it was 6:49 pm. Candice had to leave to get Gabriel and my mom stayed because she wanted to see me. Tamarah was here also. My mom and Tamarah lovingly and gently helped me to get comfortable in my room. Tamarah helped me get some water. I felt so dehydrated. Neish and Tamika drove up to the hospital and took my mom home after she was able to visit.

I was in a great deal of pain. The morphine did absolutely nothing for me so they put me on Dilaudid. That wasn't much of a help either. They upped the dose but still, nothing. So I just dealt with it. I hate that they ask me to rate the pain from 1-10. It's a 20 dammit! It hurts! I'm in pain!

Something happened with the IV in my left hand so now my hand and lower arm is swollen. Because of the IV malfunction (mishap), I was not hooked up to any fluids or pain medication (which wasn't working anyway). I can only have needles and blood pressure on my left side because lymph nodes were removed from the right. So, Kirsten, my nurse, had Ruth, another nurse find a vein. Apparently Ruth is known as one of the best. However, Ruth stuck me approximately 6-8 times because she was having a hard time finding a vein because of the excessive swelling in my arm. I was pretty sore by the time they found the vein from all of the sticks from the needle. They gave me Percocet to help with the pain until I was hooked up to some pain meds. That did nothing but made me nauseous.

Kerstin was an absolute doll. She catered to my every need. She was warm and pleasant. I wanted to bathe this morning, but found myself struggling with the six drains, the IV pole, the catheter, and partially open gown. She put a chair in the bathroom and in front of the sink and covered the seat with a cloth so I could sit comfortably. She adjusted the cords and tubes so I could free my hands and gathered all my bath necessities. After I washed the areas I could reach, she took over and washed the areas I couldn't.

She said my sink bath was the best she's seen since working as a nurse. I asked why, thinking that's how everyone would do it if they couldn't get in the tub or shower. She said my sink bath was almost like being in the shower. I was so fresh and clean. "Most people," she said, "just rub a damp cloth across themselves." Ewe! Nasty! I wanted that sick medicated smell off of me. I wanted to feel clean; refreshed.

I was finally given solid food this evening; the first solid since Thursday night. I had veggie lasagna, broccoli, a dinner roll and salad.

Been dozing on and off all day. Probably tired because I was awake most of the night, unable to sleep from the pain and discomfort. Hope to sleep better tonight.

I've been itching all over. I think it's the pain medication. It's driving me crazy! I wish I would have packed a back scratcher. I asked for a Benadryl. It helped a little.

They are giving me doses of Vancomycin (antibiotic) to prevent infection. Lord knows I don't need to go through that again.

August 24, 2008 The Next Day...

I am extremely irritable! The surgical bra they put on me is squeezing the drains which is causing them to press into my skin so I requested a bigger bra.

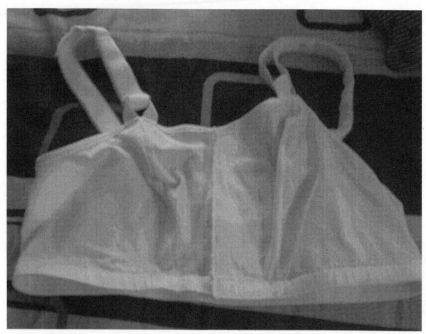

No Kerstin this morning so it took me almost an hour to wash myself up. I am in so much pain and discomfort. The new nurse is not as warm spirited as Kerstin. So, I didn't feel like bonding enough to feel comfortable with her washing me as Kerstin did. Kerstin spoiled me.

The plastic surgeon who assisted Dr. Wu said I am expected to go home tomorrow. It was possible for me to go home this evening since I was demanding it. I'm ready to go. I miss my babies.

Taylor called me around three o'clock this morning, crying. Her dad said she kept saying she was missing me and was worried about me. Since I couldn't sleep much anyway, we talked for a while. I assured her that everything was going to be fine and I would be home soon.

Being discharged from the hospital with the following prescriptions: Dilaudid, Colace (stool softener), and Bactrim (anti-biotic).

August 25, 2008 First Look, The firm, Medical Bills

My mom kept saying that Dr. Wu said she wanted to take her time with me because she was aware of how much I've been through. She said she wanted me to be happy with the results.

Came home yesterday. The ride home was a little painful, but I made it. It was a rough night. I am in so much pain. The Dilaudid still isn't working. I tossed and turned all night. I was unable to sleep. I tried over and over to reposition myself. It's painful to lie on my back, front or sides.

This morning I piled pillows high under my head to take some of the pressure off of my back. It was easier at the hospital because I could simply readjust the bed.

Shani, Michael, Terren, my mom and Candice came to see me at the hospital before I left, yesterday. Troy, Debbie, Donald, Bianka and Pat have been calling and checking in.

My mom will be here today to help me. Candice made eggs, toast, coffee and orange juice this morning before she left for work. I could only eat and drink half of almost everything. Appetite still building back up, but I needed enough in my stomach so I could take some meds.

Neish came over this morning, surprising me with a visit. She helped my mom bathe me; made lunch and assured I took all of my medication for that morning and afternoon. She said she'll be back again Thursday to stay the night and help out.

Took a look at Dr. Wu's work today. So far, so good. Looks like she took her time and did a nice job. Neisha and my mom changed all of my bandages after cleaning the site and took a couple of pictures for my journal.

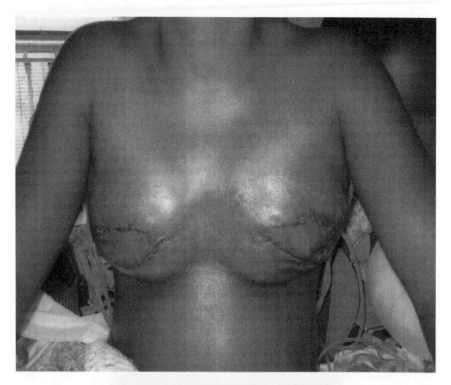

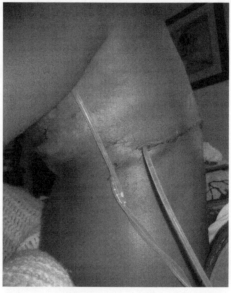

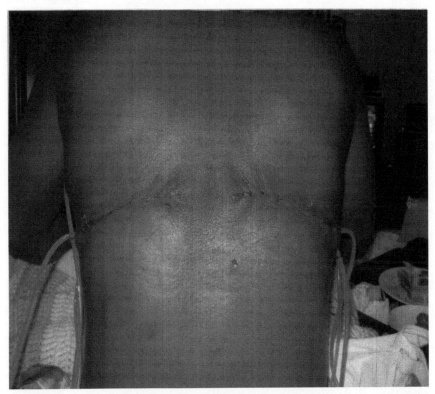

HR sent me an email saying she had a check cut for me which would cover the bills I received and reimbursement for what I paid. I was informed that some of the co-pays were the responsibility of the firm. God is good! I needed that money too and was trying to figure out how I was going to dig myself out of this financial medical debt.

August 27, 2008 Nausea, Follow-up with Oncologist

Threw up this morning. I don't think I had enough food in my stomach when I took my medication. Candice brought up some oatmeal and orange juice before she headed to work. My appetite has been off so as soon as I start eating I feel full or nauseous. I started drinking the nutrition drinks again since I can't keep much food down. I weigh 134 lbs. Yeah!

Had a follow-up with Dr. Domchek, Dr. Finley and Robin. It was so nice to see them. They gave me a warm welcome and we talked about the week in Ventnor. I thanked them again for nominating me for such a treat.

Robin went over my current meds and blood work was done. They asked how my body was responding to the Tamoxifen. No side effects as of yet. Dr. Domchek looked me over. She said everything was looking really well. She asked if I decided to go with Dr. Wu. She was very pleased when I told her I did. She assured me that Dr. Wu will take good care of me.

Dr. Domchek said since I'm high risk (BRCA1 positive), she wants me to begin screenings for ovarian cancer. My next follow-up I will have a CA125 blood test.

August 28, 2008 Still Getting Sick

Still vomiting. My mom called Dr. Wu's office. They told me to stop the Dilaudid. It might be too much for my stomach. They called Rite Aid and prescribed Vicodin (another pain med) and suppositories (to stop the nausea).

Kids took good care of me today. Joey and Taylor cleaned the house, ran my bath and we watched Family Guy for some laughs. (So inappropriate)

We've done a lot of bonding these days and it's bringing us much closer.

August 29, 2008 The Assistance and Support of Family & Friends, Drains Removed

Taylor, Joey and his friend Thomas made breakfast this morning. Kids in the kitchen. Have mercy. Actually, the pancakes and eggs they made were quite appetizing.

Neish came over last night. I kept drifting off to sleep, but she did what she could to help out as much as possible. Aunt Mopie sent over a large container of her delicious spaghetti. Another meal I wouldn't have to worry about.

The kid's father is here. He plans to stay for a couple days. He's cut the grass, washed the car, is helping with meals and is staying on top of the kids making sure they are doing what they are supposed to do.

Today, four of the six drains were removed. Rachael, the nurse practitioner talked me through each one. She told me to breathe in deep then exhale as she pulled each drain out. I could feel it sliding under my skin. It doesn't so much hurt, but it is uncomfortable- stings a little. And you can hear it. Ugh! It's an unpleasant thing to endure.

Having most of the drains removed brought some relief. The drains are so uncomfortable. It feels like someone put cords around my back, pressed on my chest as they pulled the cords tighter. It's as if I can feel them digging into my muscles from underneath my skin.

August 30, 2008 Relief, Another Bill

First bowel movement since Thursday before surgery. Pain meds make me so constipated. May need to double up on the stool softeners.

Laid on my stomach for the first time in a long time. It was very comfortable. It wasn't painful.

Candice says my breast size is nice already, despite the swelling. I want these "girls" to be sitting as high as my chin after all I've been through. I plan to talk to the doctor to see what she suggests as far as size. Since I had to endure all of this, I am going to make sure I am happy with the end result. These girls better get noticed.

August 31, 2008 St. John's Lutheran Church, Ambler

My mom's new church sent me a beautiful bouquet of flowers today. The pastor, Sandra Ellis-Killian, has called me almost every day, since I've been in the hospital, to offer me encouragement and prayer.

September 1, 2008 Questions When I Have a Follow-up with Dr. Wu

1. Can she measure me?
2. How is the expander to implant procedure performed?
3. Where is the incision made?
4. Approximately how often will I come in for injections?
5. Approximately how long until final results?
6. When can I go swimming or biking?

Must be under 30cc in a 48 hour period in order for drains to be removed

Date	Time	Drain 1	Drain 2	Drain 3	Drain 4	Drain 5	Drain 6
8/24	9 pm	19cc	20cc	18cc	22cc	18cc	20cc
8/25	10 am	21cc	30cc	20cc	20cc	20cc	20cc
8/25	11 am	20cc	30cc	15cc	20cc	20cc	30cc
8/26	11 am	20cc	25cc	15cc	10cc	20cc	20cc
8/26	10 pm	10cc	20cc	10cc	20cc	15cc	18cc
8/27	11:30 am	10cc	20cc	10cc	10cc	10cc	20cc

September 3, 2008 Draining, Blood Work

Spoke with Dr. Wu's office. They said I am still draining too much on the right side. She asked if I was right handed. I said yes. She told me whatever I was doing with my right hand, stop. I'm doing too much with my right side. If I take it easy, the draining will subside. No lifting, pulling, scrubbing my scalp. She said it should be fine by Friday and scheduled me for 11:00 am to have the last two removed. She said they don't want the drains in too long because they are a source for infection.

Robin called a couple of days ago. She said my blood work came back and everything looks great. Only concern is that my calcium level was slightly low. I have to take supplements and they will retest when I come in for my next follow-up.

September 5, 2008 Last Two Drains Removed

Where is Rachael?! I didn't like the way this woman removed the drains. She seemed to take her time like she couldn't or was scared to remove them or something. I was annoyed but relieved when it was over. I just feel tightness, like a pulling, at the incision sites. No pain though. Relief!

I was told to use Dial because the moisturizers in other soaps could get in the incision site and cause infection. I've been using Dove since I left the hospital. Now someone mentions this to me? Anyway, I have been putting 100% pure aloe (thanks Will) on my scars and they are healing nicely. I've also been using the silver sulfadiazine cream to prevent infections.

The nurse told me I didn't have to use the bandages. Just keep the sites clean and use a topical antibacterial cream.

I haven't been taking any pain medication for some time now. The discomfort has been tolerable.

September 8, 2008 Pain

Been feeling a sharp pain in my left breast. It comes and it goes. Candice looked at it. She didn't notice any swelling or bruising so she encouraged me to take it easy as to not irritate it any more than it is. I'm trying not to worry.

September 14, 2008 Another Moment at CCC

Went to The Church of Christian Compassion today. After Pastor Herndon did a sermon on judging, he made a demand for the congregation to no longer judge people on their outer appearances. He looks in my direction, "Child of God, can you come forward?" He says to me that I looked beautiful and turns to the congregation. He says to them, "Remember, some time ago, Tyesha came to the front, we shared her story as she stood here, no eyebrows and wearing a scarf, no hair. Now look at her. Can you tell what she's been through? How could you judge her or anyone else when you don't know their story?"

He called another woman up. She was recently diagnosed with cancer. Pastor said to her that I have mighty work to do in the Lord and that the Lord has so much in store for me which is why I overcame this condition. He told her to look to me for inspiration. I embraced her, we prayed with her, other survivors came forward and prayed.

When we finished, another woman grabbed me and said she wanted to share her story with me. She was 17 when she was diagnosed. She's now 34. She said after awhile, when they thought she'd be losing her life, there were no traces of cancer.

September 15, 2008 Follow-up with Dr. Wu, Menstrual Cycle

I met with Dr. Wu today. She said she kept in mind all I've been through. She said she thought I was a beautiful woman and she wanted to take her time with me. She wanted me to be happy with the results. She said she referred to me as her "Labor of Love".

She removed the remaining staples. All I felt was a pinch. She said I was healing beautifully and proceeded to expand each breast 60cc which took me to a total of 240 cc's each side. It was a small needle through the breasts skin and muscle. She pumps the saline into the expander. There was little bleeding, but I felt no pain. She suggested I go home and take a pain med just in case. She said it's possible I may not feel anything. It felt weird when she was injecting the saline. I could feel the skin stretching. She said right now, I'm probably about a small B. Candice swears I'm bigger. Dr. Wu asked me what I was aiming for. She told me I can come in once a week for the next few weeks. Then a month after the last expansion, I will be scheduled to get the expanders removed and the implants inserted. The incision will be made on the breasts where there was a previous incision. It is an outpatient procedure so I go home the same day, but need a two week recovery period. We will then discuss nipple reconstruction, which I hear is nothing.

I asked her why an expander is used and how come an implant can't be inserted right after a mastectomy. She said the implant isn't used because it prevents infection, and the results look better. She said the implant can be inserted after a mastectomy, but she is completely against it. She said it's more risk of infection and sometimes the skin is not durable enough at the time of surgery (mastectomy). It's called one step or one stop procedure. Something like that. But women have the option of getting immediate or delayed reconstruction. Although it is a discretionary procedure, doctors may still make recommendations based on the patient's situation.

She said I can resume activity (swimming & biking) six weeks from my surgery date. I can't wait.

I have signs of my menstrual cycle starting. I was spotting this morning. It's bittersweet. I'm glad to see my body getting back to "normal", but ugh, menstrual cycles.

September 16, 2008 Email to HR and
Charles Regarding my Return to Work

Good morning,

I met with my doctor yesterday. I was given clearance to return to work, with limitations (no heavy lifting, pulling, etc.) However, I still have one more surgery which will require a two week recovery period. This will be scheduled later this year. From what I understand, I will have five vacation days remaining when I return to work and I will use them for my recovery period. I will do my best to schedule my surgery on a Friday so I can also have the weekend.

You know me, I plan to push it and come back doing my full eight hour schedule. (I've been advised to take it slow and start with a half day or six hours). I believe as long as I can take it as easy as possible, while still managing my workload, I can pull it off.

That said, my return date will be September 29th.

Again, I thank you (the firm) for all of your support. You have been amazing throughout all of this. Looking forward to working with you all again.

Warm regards,

Tyesha

September 17, 2008 Email from Chele

"Hi Ty!

I just finished my lunch hour and while on lunch, I was reading the articles in Ebony.

I came across Robin Roberts', co-anchor on Good Morning America, article about her ordeal with breast cancer. OMG! It was soooooooooooo touching.

Of course I sat there and cried and thought about you, Mom, my stepmom and women in general who have gone, or are going, through this.

I am so proud that she came out publicly on television to share her news.

As for you, I truly pray that you decide as well to go public with your journal. As Robin's Mom said, "Your mess is your message."

In other words, your test is your testimony so share it if the Lord leads you because I know it will bless those your age and younger.

Ty, I love you, so keep on being the precious blessing that you are.

Take care of yourself and know I'm looking forward to your return!

Go to www.abcnews.go.com/GMA/BeautySecrets/ story?id=4694536&page=1

You'll see Robin ditch her wig at the fashion during Fashion week. :) She is truly an inspiration.

Michele Rene' Steele"

September 18, 2008 Reactions to Scars, Thinking back, Curiosity, Hair

I never did experience any pain from the expansion.

Seeing the different reactions when people see the scars on my back has been interesting. Audrey didn't say anything for a long time as she cleaned and put cream on my scars and carefully placed the bandages. She then gave me an example of how she thought it'd look when I was healed, only after I asked her opinion.

On a few occasions, Kelly, squeamishly, and Debbie, as if a wound care connoisseur, cleaned my sites and carefully placed my scar therapy pads on my back.

My brother, Michael, cleaned my back in silence. He was so gentle and loving. His girlfriend whispered a soft, "poor baby." My son said it's healing nicely. He's been so sweet caring for my back the last couple of days. My mom says I'm healing nicely. My daughter…well, she said, "Ill." Sigh.

When I think back to my doubts about getting reconstruction, I am glad I decided to go through with it. I am happy with the results thus far. I am not even fazed about not having nipples. I just love how I am looking in my clothes now. I may or may not go through with nipple reconstruction. It's not like I'll be able to feel anything anyway.

I think it's important to take several things into consideration when contemplating whether or not to go through with a mastectomy/reconstruction: Know all of your options, educate yourself. Make your own decision(s). Don't be pressured by doctors, family or friends. It's your body. A body you'll have to live with. Make the decision(s) you are most comfortable with. Doctors are specialized in the field, but ultimately, it's your decision. I opted to have it done because I carry the BRCA1 gene and didn't want to risk recurrence in my breast. In my opinion, if you opt to get a mastectomy, have both done at the same time. It won't be a delay in the final result. It's more of a chance that everything will be symmetrical and there's less time away (hospital stays) from work/school/family, etc. vs. having one done at a time.

My mom and I were having a conversation about nipple reconstruction. She told me to think of the size I want my nipples and areola in case I consider going through with it. I didn't even think about that. It would be fun to create my ideal nipple and areola size. Where do I begin researching? Lol.

I expect people to be curious about my breasts, the process, how they look. I've actually shown my brother's girlfriend, a friend and even my dad. Funny, I don't have a problem showing people. I guess I am just proud of how far I've come and the results. I didn't know what to expect going with Dr. Wu after all I've been through.

I can't recall if I mentioned the spirometer. It measures the lungs air flow. It helps patients improve the functioning of their lungs. With each surgery, I was told to do this breathing exercise several times a day.

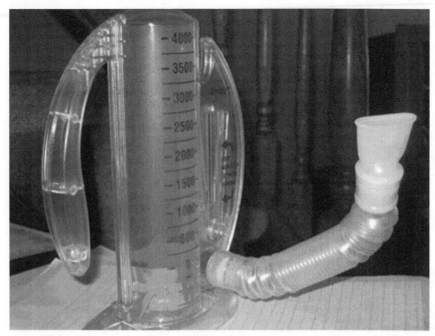

My hair is coming in beautifully and it's coming in fast. It's so soft. I hope it stays like this. Keeping it shaped up. I get so many compliments on it. People are always stopping me to say how much they love my hair. Everyone is always rubbing their hand across my hair to feel it. I love that I can shower, wet it, shuffle my fingers through the top, brush the sides and go.

September 21, 2008 Scar Therapy

I have been using Curad Scar Therapy Pads. It takes two pads each side to cover my scars. Says best results are seen after 3-4 weeks. It's recommended that pads be worn for approximately 12 hours per day. I put them on early evening so I could remove them, clean my scars/wounds and put aloe on it in the morning.

There are many scar therapy creams and pads available in drug stores. I also looked into Mederma and Scaraway. They can be a bit pricey, running from approximately $18.00-$50.00 per box. Curad had 21 pads in the pack for $20.00, if I remember correctly.

September 22, 2008 Second Expansion, Follow-up with Dr. Wu

Dr. Wu says I look really good. Says I am healing nicely. I asked her about the scar therapy pads. Says they can't hurt. So she gave me permission to continue using them.

She injected another 60cc's into each side. Takes me to 300cc's for each breast. She said I am more than half way to my goal size. I could feel a small pinch on the right side during the injection this time, but the discomfort faded quickly. I could feel my skin expanding. If you looked close enough, you could see it getting bigger; rising.

Dr. Wu said if I don't experience any discomfort we can increase the amount of the next injection. She said it's no rush, whatever I'm comfortable with.

September 23, 2008 Reflecting Back, Young Survivors Coalition

"The Young Survival Coalition (YSC) is the premier international, nonprofit network of breast cancer survivors and supporters dedicated to the concerns and issues that are unique to young women and breast cancer. Through action, advocacy and awareness, the YSC seeks to educate the medical, research, breast cancer and legislative communities and to persuade them to address breast cancer in women 40 and under. The YSC also serves as a point of contact for young women living with breast cancer." **http://www.youngsurvival.org/** Retrieved September 23, 2008

This is an amazing website. I spent a lot of time on this website after my diagnosis. It was extremely informative. I went through so many emotions while visiting the website. The women on the site are very enlightening, warm, supportive, encouraging and compassionate. I've established a couple friendships with other women who've been diagnosed with breast cancer at youthful ages. Some stories left me feeling hopeful; some left me feeling afraid. Although I'd wish this on no one, it was comforting knowing I wasn't the only one going through this. It's been therapeutic sharing stories, swapping advice and coping strategies. I've learned from, laughed with, cried; prayed for and with these women.

What saddens me, besides knowing the stories of some of these women, was to hear how long-term boyfriends/partners and husbands leave during the woman's fight with cancer. I can understand the strain that cancer can cause on the relationship – intimacy issues, being dependent on others, not being the person your significant other is used to, etc. It's a trying experience for everyone close to the survivor. It just upsets me to know that the one person you think you can count on; the one person you are supposed to be able to depend on (for better or freaking worse!), can walk out of your life at such a time when you need them most. Not only does a survivor need their significant other to help care for him/her, but for their support, encouragement, love, companionship, etc. I just can't imagine the emotional pain (on second thought, I can) the survivor feels on top of what they are going through physically when the person that vowed to always love and cherish them walks out of their life.

September 29, 2008 Appointment with Dr. Wu, Third Expansion

Dr. Wu injected another 60 cc's, totaling 360 cc's for each breast. She marks the area of the breast where the injection will occur. Bandages are placed afterwards. There has been little bleeding after the injection. She suggested three more expansions. She said I will look bigger than what I'll actually be, over the next couple expansions. She mentioned it will be more natural and less swollen after insertion of the implants. I felt that same "pinch" on the right side again.

Dr. Wu and I discussed that nipple/areola construction will take place approximately three months after the last surgery (when expanders are removed and implants are put in place).

Dr. Wu asked if I wanted silicone gel-filled or saline implants. I asked her opinion, although my mind was made up, and decided to go with silicone. She said they look and feel more natural. She gave me an information pamphlet to review and sign.

My next two expansions will be with Rachael, the Nurse Practitioner. Dr. Wu will be on vacation. I will schedule my appointment for surgery for four weeks after my last expansion which is October 20th.

October 1, 2008 Back to Work

I received a big warm welcome back to work. My workstation was decorated with flowers, balloons, signs and streamers welcoming me back, celebrating my victory and honoring me (breast cancer awareness month). My room flooded with visits from the time I got in until the time I left for the day. Mark, one of my attorneys, said, "I know you are hearing it's good to have you back, and it is. Not just because the work you do, but because it's good to have Tyesha Love back in the office." Ray, IT, said, "It's good to have you back, but it's better to know that you've gotten through that ordeal. It's good to see you getting back to yourself." I was so moved.

Charles, my supervisor, treated Kelly, Michele, Jack, Julio and me to lunch to celebrate my return.

October 4, 2008 First Hair Cut (Trim)

Candice and Shan said I was in desperate need of a trim because my hair was getting out of control. Always something to comment about. Shan and I drove to a couple of places until we came across the Hair Cuttery in Lansdale. I was nervous about someone cutting my hair since its started growing back in. It was soft and silky like hair on a newborn baby. Hesitantly, I walked inside and was greeted with a big smile by Rachel, one of the stylists. She took my name, told me to have a seat and asked what I was aiming for. I briefed her on my story and told her she should feel honored as she was the first to cut & style my hair since it's grown back in. She hugged me, gave praise for my recovery and proceeded with excitement. She trimmed, moussed and teased my hair. Thanks, Rachel, for taking such good care of my hair.

October 6, 2008 Appointment with Rachael, Dr. Wu's Nurse Practitioner, Fourth Expansion, Explanation of Benefits

Appointment went well. Injected another 60cc's so that takes me to 420 cc's in each breast. Rachael says Dr. Wu likes to reach 500cc's for a C cup. Says they expand a little bigger so that when the implant is inserted, it will have the room and will be able to take on the form of a real breast with the natural droop at the bottom. They won't look so much like pineapples (they really do look like the shape of a pineapple) sitting on my chest. She said I should be experiencing some feeling coming back and explained that not all people get the sexually stimulating (erogenous) sensation, but some get the tactile feeling back. She said whatever feeling I get back within the year is the long-term (permanent) feeling I'm expected to have. Says everything looks good. I was concerned about the scars on my back and that they were raised. She said they're still a little inflamed, but should lower and soften up. She said I should be concerned if they are soft and raised cause that would pretty much be my end result. She said give it more time. Whew!

Rachael pulled out samples of the expanders and implants for me to take pictures of.

1) The expander with the internal port. The needle penetrates the port and the saline is injected. 2) The saline implant lacked in quality (my opinion). Rachael also pointed out that the ripples in the saline implant also shows after the implant is put in place keeping it from looking completely natural. She said that it's ok for breast augmentation, but the results are different for someone getting reconstruction after a mastectomy. 3) The silicone gel-filled implant felt natural and did not show the ripple. It was well rounded, when held upright, and felt soft like a natural breast. 4) Is a picture of all three laying on a flat surface. 5) Is the needle and sterile tubing which holds the saline to be injected into the expander.

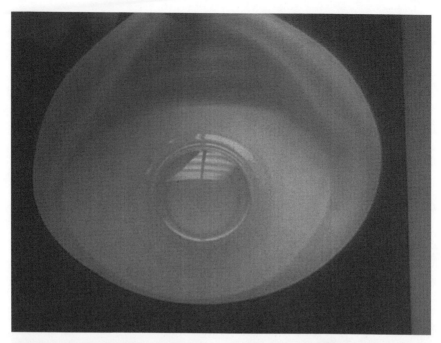

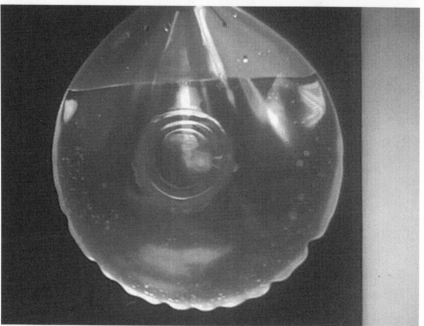

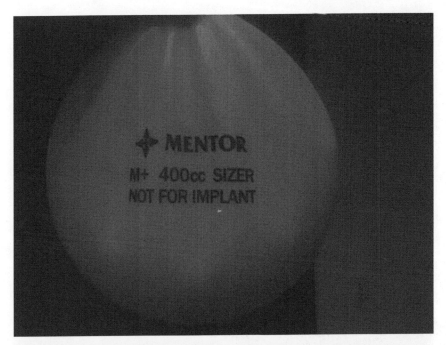

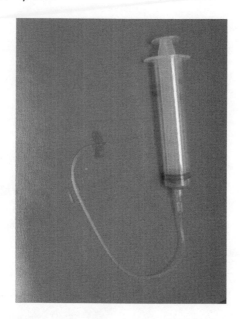

October 7, 2008 Discomfort

Felt a little discomfort in the left breast. Rachael assured me it's just from the expansion process and it's normal. I guess, since I haven't had any discomfort until now, I was a little concerned. I took some Tylenol with Codeine and it began to ease shortly after.

October 13, 2008 Making Strides Against Breast Cancer, Fifth Expansion, Don't Let Pride Block a Blessing, How Did I Feel About My Sister's BRCA1 Results

Shan and I went to the "Making Strides Against Breast Cancer" walk yesterday. Saw the First Lady of The Church of Christian Compassion, Sister Kim Herndon and Latoya, a member. Both gave me a big warm hug; said I was in their thoughts and that they hoped they would see me at the event. It was great seeing so many people out supporting and fighting to bring awareness and to raise money for a cure. I walked over to the "Survivor's Tent" and was given a t-shirt, buttons and a medal from the American Cancer Society that said "Survivor." Of course, me and my sensitive and emotional soul, I began to cry and had to excuse myself because the ladies were trying to get my registration information for next year's event. I tried to explain to Shan what I was feeling. It was a joy seeing so many out; supporting. It was a joy for having won the fight. It was sadness to think that I was even diagnosed with cancer. I had cancer...I had breast cancer...

Rachael injected another 60cc's. No pinch this time, same stretchy feeling. Shortly after, I could feel the discomfort in the left side. I took some pain meds, but it helped only a little. I plan to take something stronger tonight. It also gets uncomfortable at night after I've slept on my stomach (chest) for a while. I have been experiencing some discomfort in both breasts, but after lying on my back for awhile, it began to ease. Rachael says everything looks pretty good. I see Dr. Wu next week for the last expansion (thank God) and to discuss surgery.

I was having a discussion with Shan about how my pride blocked some of my blessings. Many people would ask what I needed; if they could bring me anything. A lot of times I'd say, "I'm fine. I don't need anything. I can't think of anything." There are so many things that can be extremely helpful when you are fighting for your health and are on a fixed income. Some suggestions are to ask for a gift card to your local market. Ask for a gas card. These come in handy for all of those trips to the doctors. A gift card to your pharmacy helps with personal needs/prescriptions.

Thinking back: I remember when my sister called to tell me her BRCA results came back negative. My lips said, "I'm so happy to hear that. I am so happy you don't have to worry about being high risk," and in my heart, I meant it. The anger in me screamed, "Why am *I* positive. Why me? How come I have to be the one to carry the gene with the risk of passing it to my offspring?" Not that I would want anyone to endure what I have, but I was so angry because I wanted to know WHY ME! I felt guilty for even having felt that way so I only shared that with two people. I needed to vent and get it off of my chest. When you are tested for the gene, they will tell you whether the results are positive or negative. You may experience mixed emotions, this is normal, but still, an unpleasant feeling.

October 14, 2008 The Breathing Room Foundation, Inc.

I came home to an envelope from The Breathing Room Foundation. It stated that they would like to relieve me of some of the financial burden and stress the holidays can bring and want to offer help in fulfilling some of the wishes the children and I have for the holiday season. The letter offers praise for my bravery and strength. Included was a holiday questionnaire, a wish list sheet and an invitation to a Holiday Festival to be held early December in Jenkintown, PA.

The emotional person I am, my eyes filled with tears and my heart filled with joy and excitement. I gathered the children at the dinner table, asked them what was on their holiday wish list and told them about the blessing from the BRF. The questionnaire also asked us to list our favorite stores, family activities and favorite restaurants.

October 15, 2008 Crossing the Finish Line, Living Beyond Breast Cancer, Chemo Brain Online Conference

Wow! Came home to another invitation. CFL sent my children, caregiver and me an invitation to their 6th Annual CFL Sailor Reception held early December in Conshohocken, PA. This is so exciting!

LBBC sent me an invitation to the News You Can Use (Breast Cancer Updates & Insights) Conference which will be held at the Pennsylvania Convention Center in Philadelphia on November 1st. It's an all day event (8:00 am – 6:00 pm) Some of the workshop sessions and presentations I'm looking forward to are: *Exploring the Genetic Connections, Creative Coping: Journaling the Breast Cancer Experience, Diet & Nutrition: Research for Breast Cancer Prevention and Risk of Recurrence, Care for Caregiver: Supporting Yourself to Support your Loved One, Long-Term Survivorship: Your Health and Well-Being.* They are also serving a continental breakfast and lunch.

The American Cancer Society had an online conference on Chemo Brain. Dr. Sledge was the guest speaker. I was surprised when I stumbled across the information for the online conference as I was researching absentmindedness related to treatment. It was enlightening as I feel I suffer this side effect from chemo.

Lately, I realized, and it has been brought to my attention, that I have been forgetting things a lot more than usual. It scares me because I am forgetting important dates; significant events in my life (past and present); to take medication, etc. Oftentimes, I don't know if I'm coming or going. I'm writing everything down. This has been a challenge, because I am usually one to remember the smallest of details. Now, I have reminders for everything, everywhere - notes on the refrigerator; all over my day planner; on my dresser and in the car. It drives me crazy. I'm driving myself crazy.

October 16, 2008 Medical Charges

I am amazed at some of the amounts billed to my insurance company. I was reviewing the itemized billing statement from the hospital and couldn't believe how much they charged for some of these things. Procedures, treatments, pills and, hospital stays cost thousands upon thousands of dollars.

October 17, 2008 Questions to ask Dr. Wu regarding Implants

- Does it make sense for me to continue to get mammograms after this?
- How concerned should I be about needing implant replacement after three years?
- Chances of rupture?
- I hear some women go 20 years before having to replace their implant. Is this true?
- Can I choose between moderate profile, moderate plus profile and high profile?
- Smooth or textured implants?

October 18, 2008 Second Hair Cut at Hair Cuttery with Rachel

Rachel seemed happy to see me. Promised her I'd bring her a copy of the picture we took together for my journal. I'm glad she was working tonight because I needed a cut badly. Seems that the shorter you keep your hair, the faster it grows. She keeps saying how "incredibly soft" it is. It's beautiful.

October 19, 2008 Discomfort

Experienced a great deal of discomfort this afternoon, but it eased after a couple pain relievers. Not sure about getting this last expansion. The discomfort is getting worse and these "girls" look huge.

October 20, 2008 Last Expansion, Surgery Scheduled

Met with Dr. Wu. She said I look really good and suggested I get one more expansion. She said I will feel huge (and I do), but assures me they will be beautiful with a natural shape when she's done with me. I was hesitant about getting another injection since I had been experiencing so much discomfort with the last two. She was adamant about giving me one more injection - another 60cc. Candice teased me telling me to put on her bra (which is bigger than my size) and I was able to fit it. OMG! I'm huge! She spent the evening taking pictures to email to Derrick (as if I'm some kind of side show freak). LOL

Speaking of Derrick. Been meaning to note, last time I came home from the hospital, Derrick brought me a beautiful bouquet of flowers and a heartening card. They were beautiful sitting in my bedroom window. They really lifted my spirits. Thank you, Derrick. That was so thoughtful.

Back to my injection: Pains kicked in a half hour after leaving the office. I popped two Tylenol with codeine and it eased fairly quickly. Relief!

My appointment for surgery has finally been scheduled. I have to come into the office November 10th to see Rachael (blood work, pre-registration) then surgery is November 20th. PERFECT! I have five vacation days left at work so I can take off November 20th - 30th to recover. With the weekend and holidays (office closed 25th and 26th), I have ample time to recover and return to work, with limitations, of course. My job already approved my time off.

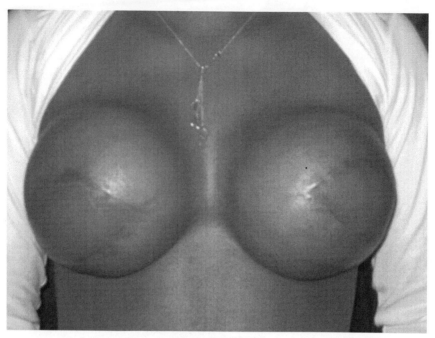

Final Expansion

October 21, 2008 Hallmark Card from Lisa Melvin

Lisa, a long time friend of the family, (so much so I consider her my aunt) sent me a card remembering me during Breast Cancer Awareness Month. Thank you for such a beautiful card. That was very thoughtful of you. Much love.

October 24, 2008 Pain, Medication, Donations, Buying Fabric for Scarves

Decided to start my day with breakfast and pain medication over the next couple of days. I figured I'd be proactive and have something in my system before the discomfort has a chance to kick in. The right side (which Dr. Wu said was slightly larger than the left) has been extremely uncomfortable (painful) over the last couple of days. But, no worries. The pain will subside and it will be symmetrical after surgery. I have so much confidence in her. She's been amazing thus far. She always says,

"Things are going so well, knock on wood. We have a ways to go with another surgery coming up, but let's stay hopeful." She's brought me a great deal of comfort and peace as I was irresolute about reconstruction after my experiences with the infections.

I decided to donate a couple of my wigs, scarves, mastectomy supplies, etc. to the Breast Cancer Center at Chestnut Hill. Amanda had items there that people donated and I figured I could help someone with some of the items I am no longer using.

I was thinking back to when I first purchased materials for my sister scarves. My mom and Shan accompanied me to Wal-mart, where material was on sale, and they had a fairly nice selection. I opted for the linen as it was approaching summer and I knew I'd want something that wasn't hot, but light and stylish. It was a bit emotional at first as it was a token of what I was about to endure (losing my hair to chemo). My mom said it's best I get them now that way I'd already have them when it came time for me to use them. She said it might be more difficult for me to try to pick fabric/scarves after my hair already started to fall out.

November 1, 2008 Living Beyond Breast Cancer's *News You Can Use* Conference

I really enjoyed the conference. I was just disappointed I could not attend more of the workshops. They had four workshops going at a time so I had to pick one from the morning sessions and one from the afternoon sessions. The sessions I chose were Creative Coping: Journaling the Breast Cancer Experience and Long-term Survivorship: Your Health and Well-Being. I would have loved to have sat in on the Exploring the Genetic Connection and Diet & Nutrition: Research for Breast Cancer Prevention and Risk of Recurrence workshops. Lunch was provided and we were given the opportunity to visit exhibitor tables while on lunch break.

I really enjoyed the Creative Coping workshop, with speaker Howard M. Rice, as I have been journaling my entire experience. Initially, my journal was simply for therapeutic reasons, then so many encouraged me to write it for others directly or indirectly afflicted with the disease. Although I hope my journal will bring insight to people about cancer, treatments, surgeries, etc., first and foremost, it was a release for me. It was my way of being able to recall what I came through. It is something for my children or other family members (since it runs heavily on my mom's side of the family) to look back on, learn from or use to be proactive with their own health.

The Long-Term Survivorship workshop explained the long-term and late effects of chemotherapy. Long-term effects that are continuous after treatment is completed, but eventually go away. Late effects manifest for months or years after treatment. We discussed side effects and ways to cope.

A Dexascan (bone scan) was highly recommended for patients finished with chemotherapy. I have to remember to ask Dr. Domchek if I should get one, especially since my calcium level was low.

The guest speaker, Dr. Linda A. Jacobs, went over the importance of developing a Survivorship Care Plan. I need to start with getting a summary of my treatments. I have to remember to ask Robin for that.

I also learned that once a cancer patient's/survivor's labs are back to normal their immune system is no longer compromised. That's a relief. I can stop spraying people with Lysol when they come around me sneezing and coughing.

At the conference, they had leis identifying time of diagnosis. If I remember correctly, orange (mine) was for those diagnosed less than a year, blue for healthcare providers, yellow for caregivers, green for those whose cancer metastasized, white for those diagnosed 1-5 years, another color for those diagnosed 6-10 years and so on.

One of the exercises from the Creative Coping workshop was to write for ten minutes. We were given three options. I chose option three which asked, "If your cancer was to walk in this room, what would it look like and what would you say to it." I focused more on what I would say to it and ran out of time before I could get all of my thoughts out. What I started to say was, "What are you doing here? It doesn't matter. Let me take this opportunity to say this. You thought you could steal my spirit, but you only made me stronger, shown me more of the beauty that life had to offer, appreciate the things that are truly meaningful and given me the desire to love and care for myself and my family more than I ever have. I must admit, there were times you had me doubting my faith and my ability to get through the treatments and surgeries.

You almost broke me. You really had me fooled. I actually wanted to give up after a few treatments, infections, hospitalization. Loved ones, faith, hope and prayer reminded me that I could beat you. These things and those in my life were much more powerful than you. My God is more powerful than you. I was reminded that you were simply a season in my life that would soon come to pass. You only grew and matured me mentally, physically, spiritually. You didn't win. You made me stronger; educated me on how to take better care of myself; influenced me to make my loved ones aware of how to better care for themselves." (Writing time was up before I could finish telling my cancer how much it didn't break me.)

November 2, 2008 People Just Don't Realize...

This thing really is not over for me. The questions, which I don't mind, make it obvious that people do not understand the severity of battling cancer; the long-term effects of battling cancer; the recovery period after battling cancer; the road to feeling "normal". Why do you still need surgery? Aren't you done with the doctors? People don't realize that my breasts are still under reconstruction. Three months after that, reconstruction for my nipples will begin, then areola tattooing. They don't realize I am a candidate for other cancer screenings, high risk for other cancers, subject to routine tests, studies, as I carry the BRCA1 gene.

November 3, 2008 Catching Up with Luff "Will"

I was catching up with Will and he asked about the kids, school, my health, etc. (as he usually does). I reminded him I had surgery coming up in a few weeks. He took this opportunity to say that there was a lot he admired about me while going through this ordeal, but one he admired most was my determination to stay in school. He said people drop out of school for trivial reasons, but I managed to stay the course. Says he admires that I was determined to continue bettering myself and furthering my education. I must say, I am proud of me. In a way, school helped take my mind off of cancer sometimes. I've had such a desire to further my education after having raised my children. It was too important for me to let go of such a goal.

November 4, 2008 Crossing the Finish Line

They sent me a disc of the pictures from our respite in Ventnor, NJ. The letter, that came with the disc, said as a CFL "sailor" we hold a special place in their community. They sent well wishes and let me know to contact them if there is anything they can do. Thank you, Mimi and Ashley. This was an amazing experience and I loved looking back on that time spent with my family.

November 6, 2008 Email from The Breathing Room Foundation

"Tyesha

I have a group of boys lacrosse players that would like to perform community service along with their coaches. They are looking to do yard work for our families. Please let me know if this would be helpful to you. They plan to come out next weekend on Saturday. They would rake and bag leaves, clear out gardens, etc. You would not need to be home at the time.

Let me know if this is something that would be helpful to you.
Mary Ellen"
The Breathing Room Foundation
www.breathingroomfoundation.org

Of course I told Mary Ellen I was excited about this opportunity. I'm sure my son will be excited as well. Yard work is his responsibility.

November 10, 2008 Pre-registration with Rachael, Final Appointment Before Surgery

I sat in the waiting room and could feel someone looking at me. I looked up from my book and a woman, with beautiful salt and pepper hair, sitting diagonally from me was staring right into my eyes. I smiled and looked at her with a puzzled look because of her stare. She apologized and said I looked familiar. I shrugged my shoulders, cocked my head and twisted my lips as if to say, "I don't know from where." She said, "Either way (whether she knows me or not), I am simply beautiful." I gave her a big smile, thanked her and told her she made my day. (I was having a rough morning). She continued to say how familiar I looked to her. I said maybe she knew me from there (the hospital). She told me she was a patient on the 14th floor (oncology) and I shared that I too was a recent patient of the 14th floor. She asked to sit next to me and we continued to swap stories. It was amazing how much Bella and I had in common. She finished her treatments a month after me and just finished with her radiation treatments. She shared in my excitement about surgery next week. We both agreed that it was horrible having these "things" as breasts. They are just so hard. We both talked about how self-conscious we were about hugging people. She said she had to get used to giving people "air hugs." She said she saw a friend she hadn't seen in a long time and she hugged him and it startled him. She said I looked great and if she didn't know I had cancer, she would not be able to tell. We talked about decisions to continue with nipple and areola construction. We discovered that we both had

Dr. "Surgeon" as a plastic surgeon at one point. (She went for another reason other than breast reconstruction). The both of us shared similar feelings regarding "Surgeon"... Our conversation was interrupted when Rachael called me to the back. Bella and I expressed that we hoped to cross paths again. It was a pleasure chatting with her. It brightened my day. She has a beautiful spirit.

Rachael also shared in my excitement about next weeks' surgery. She said, "We can finally get those hard things out of you." Hooray! We went over my current medication, filled out some paperwork and took my vitals. I had a list of questions for Rachael to help me prepare for next week.

How will I care for my breasts? I can wear a camisole. No underwire bras (not that I need a bra anyway. Haven't worn a bra for some time now. I can shower after 48 hours and will have dissolvable sutures. I just have to keep the area clean.

What are my limitations? (I was concerned with the holidays coming up. I have cooking and decorating to do). No heavy lifting and no repetitive motions (e.g. vacuuming).

Will there be a follow-up appointment? Two weeks.

Approximately how long is the surgery? About 2 hours.

Rachael told me the pain is usually compared to the worse expansion pain. I will not be coming home with drains and the incisions will be in the same location as the incision sites left after the mastectomy/ insertion of the expanders. So, no extra scars. Thank God...I already have enough.

I learned that I will go home with a surgical bra on. I will be sent home with antibiotics and pain medication. I can continue taking the calcium, Tamoxifen and vitamins. Just avoid medication with aspirin a week before surgery. Tylenol is ok.

Surgery will be at the SurgiCentre in the new Ruth and Perelman Center for Advanced Medicine. She said Dr. Wu will be sure to see me before surgery.

November 12, 2008 Taking on Too Much. Trying To Get Back To "Normal" Too Quickly. An Email from Shan

I was feeling guilty about taking time off from work again, but I was anticipating the break. I asked Shan if it was wrong for me to look forward to having the time off - primarily because I had just returned to work. Via email she responded by saying:

"This year you had a MAJOR life threatening illness of which you conquered successfully. You have had many surgeries and weeks of hospital stays. All the while, you've continued to raise two wonderful children and attend college full-time.

Our bodies can take but so much, Meek. You're now exhausted because your body has to get use to you working again on a full-time basis. This just doesn't include work, it includes getting up at 6 each morning, helping the kids at night, the pressures of the daily commute, the stresses of supporting numerous attorneys at work, and the strains of being a professional while at work......the list goes on and on............

So no, it is not wrong to feel the way you currently do. I can completely understand why you are exhausted. If I'm not mistaken, both me and Tamarah tried to plant a bug in your ear to go back to work part-time. We knew this may happen.

That said, the next few weeks may actually turn out to be a huge blessing. You have your final surgery, you'll be wrapping up the 2 classes before the Christmas holiday, and you'll have ample time to recover from the surgery - hence the much needed time off.

My suggestion: once you're finish with these 2 classes, do NOT take more than one accelerated class at a time. Never again! I tried to dissuade you from doing so prior to you agreeing to take on the communications class, but you didn't want to listen. So I supported you on your decision. It's not that I thought you couldn't do well in the class, it's just that I knew with everything else you had going on..........it was simply too much for you now Mika. (Especially since I know how well you like to perform in all your courses and how well you do when given the right opportunity).

My trying to talk you out of taking the communications class was not meant to seem negative and/or discouraging. In all honesty, I saw the rocks falling from the mountain and tried to push you out of the way. As we get older, with wisdom comes the realization that we can not do everything, be everything, or even have everything.

You are an excellent student. A wonderful and caring mother. An awesome sister and daughter. You must now learn how to be yourself. And accept yourself as you are - not who you used to be. The woman who used to multi-task ANYONE under the ground. You can only stretch yourself and your abilities, but so far before you begin to be (or appear to be) ineffective.

Try taking advantage of this much needed time off. Restructure the things around you so you can comfortably "be." If you take one course at time and graduate in 2010, that's a true blessing. Last I checked, a degree awarded in 2010 will hold the same merit as one issued in 2009.

You will be fine. You have to accept where you are with everything and, as I always say, "Start taking one day and doing one thing at a time or else you'll find yourself exhausted again and again as you are now."

November 13, 2008 Crossing the Finish Line – Yard work

CFL called to reschedule the yard cleaning for November 22nd. We are expecting heavy rains tomorrow.

November 14, 2008 Breathing Room Foundation – Thanksgiving Basket

The BRF called to schedule a date and time to drop off the basket. Sunday at 3:00 pm. First they asked me approximately how many people I expected for dinner. I'm trying to hold off food shopping until I see what I get in the basket. I did get my few things since they were on sale. I am so excited about the basket. This is truly a blessing. It relieves me of some of the holiday stress of food shopping and spending more money.

November 21, 2008 Day Before Surgery

My dad spent the entire morning with me. We laughed, had prayer, and truly enjoyed each other's company. I received plenty of calls, texts and emails from friends and family checking in to see how I was doing. I have another big day ahead of me.

November 22, 2008 Surgery - Removal of Tissue Expanders - Getting the Implants

The SurgiCentre at the new Perelman Center is coming along nicely. Shan and I arrived at 11:30 am, parked with ease and proceeded to the 3rd floor.

Artis, at the front desk, was comical. She quickly diffused the anxiety that swept over me from the time I parked till the time I reached check-in. Gwen was soft spoken. She has a reserved demeanor, but was very nice. She seemed dedicated and focused on her work. Stephanie and Jennifer took their turns prepping me for surgery. I changed into my gown, booties and cap. Linda came in to do my vitals and IV (one in the hand and the other in my arm), but had some trouble. It concerned me thinking the damage that chemo might have done to my veins. She said she didn't want to keep sticking me so she'd let the anesthesiologist do it. We chatted for a minute about President-elect Barack Obama, raising sons, education and careers. She had a warm spirit.

Michael and Justina (anesthesiologists) came over to do paperwork, go over my medical history and discuss side effects of anesthesia. Justina did my IV and I felt nothing when she pricked me as Michael had me laughing hysterically (I can't remember what about). He may have been teasing me about the last time I had eaten (11:55 pm). Yes, I pushed it to the limit. I had three dinners last night.

Dr. Wu came in to see me. Says I look voluptuous. ☺ She took some before pictures of my breasts and my back; then she marked me for surgery. She says everything is symmetrical except for the nipple area which she can't do much about since the scar was what was left after the mastectomy.

Everything moved along quickly. I thought I would sit around waiting, but before I knew it, they told me my room was ready and it was time. Shan gave me that *everything is going to be okay* look as they pushed me down the hall. Anxiety kicked in as soon as I saw the operating table (always does). I guess it was all over my face. Michael said he was going to get me situated and give me a cocktail. He asked if I felt anything, which I didn't, so he offered me another. I accepted and that one did the trick. I felt groovy. By this time, I was already emotional and fearful of going through yet another surgery and not knowing what was to come. One of the other assistants stood by my side, held my hand and talked to me about what I've come through; asked me if I planned to get nipple and areola reconstruction. We talked about how wonderful Dr. Wu is and next thing I know, I was waking up in the recovery room. Done! I have boobies!

I felt little pain. More of an ache. Nothing like what I experienced with previous procedures. I did still feel a little drowsy. I was offered crackers and apple juice and the t.v. was turned on. News…depressing news. I didn't have the energy to change the channel. Shan came to the back and asked me how I felt. We sat there for about an hour and a half before we left. I was given an ice pack, discharge instructions (have to make a one week follow-up appointment), and id card for my implants (has the name of the implant, model number, serial number, lot numbers and Mentor contact information). I was also given a prescription for Bactrim (antibiotic), Percocet (pain relief) and Bacitracin (ointment). The Bacitracin was not covered under my insurance, but it was only $4.99 over the counter. I also came home with bandages over the incisions and a surgical bra.

I took the Percocet for a while, but stopped and started taking extra strength Tylenol. Every time I would take the Percocet, after awhile, I'd start vomiting and would be extremely drowsy.

November 23, 2008 CFL - Yard work

CFL sent a group of about 20 guys to the house to do yard work. It was amazing. They pulled up in three vehicles, one with a trailer that held lawn mowers, rakes, blowers, brooms, trash bags, etc. They blew leaves, raked and swept. It was so exciting and it happened so fast. Rich, one of the team leaders, even offered to fix my screen door for me. He sent someone to the hardware store, bought a new fixture and fixed the handle and latch. They were so nice and extremely helpful.

Email to Mary Ellen:

I wanted to take a moment to say that the team of guys you sent were simply wonderful. They did an amazing job. They were extremely generous, even offering to fix things that weren't on the agenda. Seeing them work as a team to assist others, who may not have the energy, time, or strength to do yard work, was touching. I was truly moved.

Thank you for having the guys come by. Every little thing is a help and this was truly another blessing The Breathing Room Foundation has sent my way.

Kind regards,
Tyesha

November 23, 2008 BRF - Thanksgiving Basket

I was sitting here baking cookies with Taylor when the door bell rang at exactly 3:00 pm, as scheduled. Raymond and two others delivered a basket of food from Grace Presbyterian Church in Abington. The label said it was packed by Susan and Grace. They came in with a large box and two bags. One held a 21lb turkey; the other bag was a sweet potato pie, apple pie and a pumpkin pie. In the box were macaroni and cheese, cranberry sauce, potatoes, veggies, biscuits, bread, stuffing, cake mix, frosting, whipped cream, butter, gravy, plates, napkins, sweet potatoes and a roasting pan. I am so excited about this blessing that will allow me to enjoy the holidays stress free.

November 28, 2008 Healing Nicely

I'm healing fairly quickly and recovering well. Getting my energy and appetite back and I haven't taken any pain meds for a few days now. The swelling has gone down and my breasts are softening up. It's a nice change from them feeling as hard as cantaloupes. I'll be well enough to go back to work this Monday.

About two days ago, I changed my mind again about getting the nipple and areola reconstruction. I was looking in the mirror at my "new breasts" and was thinking of the positions of the incision sites (scars). I'm hoping they lighten up a bit. I plan to get some scar therapy pads and use them on my breasts and see how well the scars fade. The pads have done a wonderful job on my back. Then I will make a decision of whether or not I think it's worth it for me to get the nipple and areola. I guess I can discuss it with Dr. Wu during my follow-up appointment.

December 2, 2008 Crossing the Finish Line, Sailor Reception

The reception was held in a church in Conshohocken. Beautifully decorated tables with poinsettia center pieces filled the room. The tree stood bright and tall in one of the corners stealing the attention of everyone entering the room. Name tags were provided and a picture was taken of the sailor and their family members. I met and took pictures with Marci, president and founder of CFL. I kept thanking her for all she's done for my family and the many families she's assisted that have been faced with cancer. I met many of those who donate their homes for CFL sailors. I was moved by all those that support CFL and touched by those in their battles. We had a delicious dinner and inspiring conversations. The kids, Shan and I had a memorable experience with encouraging stories shared. We ended the night with group pictures (sailors and donators). Everyone went home with a beautiful poinsettia.

Joe, Me, Tay, Shan

December 6, 2008 Breathing Room Foundation, Holiday Festival

The festival was held at Grace Presbyterian Church in Jenkintown. Mary Ellen greeted us at the door and gave the kids two tickets to use as money to buy gifts from a table set up in the church. They offered a nice selection of gifts for men, women and children. The kids liked the idea of being able to shop for Christmas presents.

Another table was set up for girls to make bracelets, another for kids to make stuffed animals complete with a heart (to stuff inside) and a shirt for their fluffy friend. There was also a table set up for arts and crafts.

Santa came in and the children went wild with excitement. They all took turns taking pictures with Santa and telling him their Christmas wish list. I managed to get my children to at least take a picture. They thought they were too big for that.

Tables were arranged banquet style and they served pizza, hoagies, wraps, cookies, pretzels, chips, cake and beverages. I scanned the room as I sat down to eat my lunch and could identify those still in treatment: hairless heads covered, distressed, pale faces, weakness in the way they walked. In these folks, I saw how I looked earlier this year.

As I left, Mary Ellen said I would be hearing from her soon regarding our wish list. I'm so excited.

December 8, 2008 Follow-up with Dr. Wu and Dr. Domchek

She says I look really nice and healed real well. She gave me a wrap to wear for the next two weeks to push my breasts down to give them a natural droop. I tried it on. It's a bit uncomfortable. It reminds me of the surgical bras so I tossed it to the side.

We talked about the nipple reconstruction and she convinced me to go through with it and get them. She says it's a simple procedure. I'll be awake, no pain, little blood and I can go to work the next day. She said she'll see me in three months.

I received a warm greeting from Dr. Domchek and Robin. It was really nice seeing them. I was emotional seeing them after having the rough part of this behind me. Visiting the office in different spirits felt so good. It was sad sitting in the waiting area seeing those who were clearly in the beginning stages of treatment.

Dr. Domchek and Robin complimented me on my reconstruction. I thanked them for referring me to Dr. Wu, as I've been so happy under her care and with her work. They couldn't believe how good I looked after what I've been through. I didn't expect my breasts to look as nice as they do. I could not envision how Dr. Wu would turn my holes into breasts.

My vitals were taken. Everything was good. My weight was 134. Sigh… I had blood drawn to check my calcium levels, iron levels and for the CA125 test. The CA125 test is an ovarian cancer screening. CA-125 is a protein found more so in ovarian cancer cells than in other cells.

Dr. Domchek asked how I was doing. I told her physically I feel fine. Still get tired from time to time, not sleeping well and told her about an emotional episode I had a couple days ago.

Reflecting back to a couple of days ago: I sat at my desk crying on and off for about two hours thinking it was just days from the anniversary date of my diagnosis. I was experiencing all of those emotions I felt when I was diagnosed. I was told it was normal and I would experience that for a couple of years, but in time will move past it as I begin to focus on my current state of health and moving beyond what I went through.

December 10, 2008 CA-125 Results

Normal! What great news to receive on the anniversary of my diagnosis.

December 19, 2008 Hair

My hair is so thick and curly. However, it's still extremely soft. Still getting many compliments on my hair. Not missing my long hair as much as I used to. My sister did mention I should, at some point, get my twists again. I'll consider it when I decide to grow my hair back. That will get me through that horrible in between stage.

December 20, 2008 Breathing Room Foundation fulfills our Christmas Wish List through Immaculate Conception School

Mary Pat and her husband delivered a box and bag of wrapped gifts from Immaculate Conception School in Jenkintown, PA. In addition, there was a stack of beautifully handmade Christmas cards. I sat on the floor, read, was moved, inspired and encouraged by each one. The kids are excited about their gifts from the BRF & ICS as they piled them under the Christmas tree.

December 22, 2008 Thank You!

I bought festive stationary and sent thank you notes to the Breathing Room Foundation, Immaculate Conception School, Grace Presbyterian School and Crossing the Finish Line. I also included family pictures with the blessings they sent our way. I was thinking about how, a few weeks ago, I was stressing about pulling off the holidays after having not worked all year. I look now and my tree is filled with gifts beneath its branches. My refrigerator is packed with food to cook for the holiday. God always proves to be faithful.

December 23, 2008 Sleeping Patterns

I have to remember to mention the changes in my sleeping patterns, at my next appointment with Dr. Wu or Dr. Domchek. I did mention to Dr. Domchek during my last appointment and she suggested a few exercises. I can't say that I have followed the exercises as directed so I am not sure as to how concerned I should be that my sleeping patterns seem to have worsened. Last night, with a sleep aid, I went to sleep at

9:00 pm, woke at 3:00 am, went back to sleep at 5:00 am, woke at 6:00 am. A couple of nights ago I woke at 4:00 am and never went back to sleep. I'm exhausted. It could be holiday stress and anxiety. It's so much going on.

January 5, 2009 Pelvic and Transvaginal Ultrasounds

When last I met with Dr. Domchek, it was recommended that I meet with at least one of my cancer doctors (oncologist: Dr. Bailey, Dr. Domchek) every three months. So, my first appointment was today at UPenn for my abdominal ultrasound and transvaginal probe.

The appointment went well for my pelvic and transvaginal ultrasounds. A little uncomfortable, pressure, but no pain. Some fibroids were found. I was told not to be alarmed. It's normal and they are benign. I may experience pain and heavy menstrual (which explains the abdominal pain I've had on and off over the last couple of weeks). I should have the results from both ultrasounds some time this week.

I had to have a full bladder, so on my way to the hospital, I forced down 32oz of water on an empty stomach. An abdominal probe works best when patients have a full bladder. The computer produces a better picture of the uterus from the sound waves when the bladder is full.

Madeline, the radiologist, explained what she was looking at/for as she proceeded with the abdominal probe. She called in Dr. Sweet to stand in for the vaginal probe. I felt like I was getting a damn pap smear. That's the part that caused the slight bit of pressure. The abdominal ultrasound wasn't too bad. Just pressing on my belly with a full bladder was uncomfortable. I was able to clear my bladder after the ultrasound and before the probe.

I mentioned to Dr. Sweet that I have been experiencing some abdominal pains. He said that can be from the fibroids and I can also experience heavy bleeding. Dr. Sweet also noted that I may experience irregular menstrual cycles for a while after chemo, which I have. My menstrual still hasn't come on yet this month. My body feels like its coming on, but still nothing.

January 6, 2009 Ultrasound Results, Robin Calls from Dr. Domchek's Office

Robin: Hi Tyesha

Me: (Recognizing her voice) Hi Robin, how are you?

Robin: I'm good, how are you?

Me: Fine, thanks.

Robin: Are you at work?

Me: Yes, WHY ROBIN?! WHAT'S WRONG?! (Fearing the worse news while recalling Dr. Bailey saying if she would have known I was at work, she would have waited to tell me about my diagnosis)

Robin says nothings wrong. She said she didn't want to alarm me, but they found a cyst on my right ovary and they want to do a short-term follow-up. She said if I did not have the gene they would not worry about it because, oftentimes, cysts can dissolve. Because I am positive for the mutation, they want to do a follow-up after two menstrual cycles between 6-10 days of the follicular phase. I am to call Trish, the receptionist, to schedule the appointment when I get my second menstrual cycle (next month if I get a regular menstrual). Robin already put the order in for the ultrasound.

My nerves are a wreck. I was panicking and worrying and then my friend Charles (Foy) says to me, "Why are you worried, Ty? Stop worrying and let God be God." Although *all* of my anxiety did not vanish, I did feel a sense of peace almost instantly. How true. God is in control of this situation. I have to focus more on Him and His control of the situation and less on the circumstance. He always proves Himself faithful. So, I'm doing the best I can to leave it in His hands.

January 15, 2009 Invitation to TWCP for a Special Event

I received a letter from Dr. Domchek inviting me to an event hosted by Abramson Cancer Center and FORCE (Facing Our Risk of Cancer Empowered - facingourrisk.org). It will be held February 21, 2009, from 3:30 pm -6:30 pm at the Wellness Community of Philadelphia. http://www.twcp.org/.

During the event, the documentary film *In the Family* will be shown. The film is about Joanna Rudnick's (award winning director and producer of the film) personal journey through genetic testing and what follows after being tested positive for the mutation. The event will have several specialists from the Cancer Risk Evaluation Program, including Dr. Domchek. They will update us on new research opportunities and exercise intervention for young women at increased risks. Following, questions can be answered with experts, including Dr. Susan Domchek - Director, Kathryn Schmitz-Epidemiologist and Exercise Physiologist, Jill Stopfer-Genetic Counselor, Jacquelyn Powers-Genetic Counselor, Robin Herzog-Oncology Nurse Practioner and Nicole Dugan and Bryan Spinelli-Cancer Rehabilitation Physical Therapists.

The event is suggested for those with family history of breast and/or ovarian cancer; family or personal history of BRCA1 or BRCA2 risk; those considering or who have had genetic testing due to family history of breast or ovarian cancer.

The Wellness Community offers services to people with cancer and to their loved ones. Services include support groups, mind body workshops, educational seminars, creative art studios, exercise classes and nutrition programs. They recently had a Young Women with Breast Cancer networking group meeting. It's in partnership with the Young Survival Coalition. I missed this one, but it's a monthly meeting so I plan to attend next month.

January 21, 2009 Menstrual Cycle, CFL, Weight Gain

Damn thing finally came on Jan. 12th. Extremely heavy flow for three days then nothing. Intense cramps (piercing pain) and achy back (not like a cramp).

CFL called to remind me of the Beach Ball Gala. I'm looking forward to this event.

I weigh 141 pounds! I'm gaining my weight back. I love being thick and curvy.

January 23, 2009 LBBC *Insight* Newsletters

I have been receiving LBBC Insight newsletters. I am just getting around to really looking at them and found them extremely insightful and informative. One newsletter listed organizations that offer free consultation and financial assistance to people with breast cancer. Some of those organizations included Partnership for Prescription Assistance (pparx.org), Patient Access Network Foundation (patientaccessnetwork. org), Patient Advocate Foundation (patientadvocate.org), CancerCare (cancercare.org/get_help), Healthwell Foundation (www. healthwellfoundation.org), HR Mehling Cancer Fund (bmcf.net), Cis B. Golder Quality of Life Grant, (CMS) Centers for Medicare and Medicaid Services (cms.hhs.gov) and National Breast and Cervical Cancer Early Detection Program (cdc.gov/cancer/nbccedp).

Reviewing the newsletter, I remembered that LBBC posted transcripts and audio recordings from LBBC conferences on the website. They also had LBBC forums. Some forums were titled Getting Connected, High Risk, Newly Diagnosed, Our Corner, LBBC Connection, The Young Survivor Connection and We Celebrate Tomorrow. I decided to take a quick glance at the latest conference transcripts that would be of interest to me and found quite a few. Some were Taking Control and Managing End-of-Life Issues, Fashion Your Best Fit: Breast Prostheses and Intimate Clothing, Ask the Expert Panel at the 6th Annual Conference for Young Women Affected by Breast Cancer, Inspired by Faith: Nurturing Your Spirit, Your New Normal: Reclaiming Body Image, Moving Beyond Breast Cancer: From Treatment to Survivorship, Restoring Energy after Treatment, Your New Normal: Moving on after Breast Cancer Treatment, Moving on: Discovering Your New Normal and The Body Beautiful: Reclaiming Body Image and Intimacy. These are just a few of the transcripts that sparked my interest. There are a plethora of transcripts from conferences that will help survivors, their loved ones, spouses, caregivers, etc. Anyone that wants or needs to learn more about the many facets of cancer, treatments, etc. will benefit from these postings.

January 25, 2009 Crossing the Finish Line's
V.I.P. Reception and Beach Ball Gala

What a beautiful evening. Marci spoke giving thanks to all those who donate their homes, monies and time which provide respites for families dealing with the daily struggles of cancer. A sailor spoke about how he would no longer be the provider for his family upon his diagnosis. He's been getting treatments for over a year now. He recalled being contacted by CFL and couldn't believe the respite they wanted to offer his family. Listening to other survivors and their stories sent me through a whirlwind of emotions. I'm sad that someone has to experience a cancer diagnosis; I'm happy that they are strong and fighting for their lives. I'm encouraged by their strength and reminded of my blessings.

Shan and I sat with Marci's mom, dad, sisters and in-laws. What a fun and convivial bunch. The Crystal Tea Room was beautifully decorated. The food was appetizing, the cosmopolitans were delish and the music (live band) was apposite and entertaining. Sitting at the table nearest the dance floor, I watched couples waltz, gracefully, in unison.

February 9, 2009 My New Normal

Recently, I had a panic attack so Shan urged to call Domchek's office. I have a lot of things going on in my life on top of my worries about the transvaginal ultrasound they want to retake. Robin calls me and began asking a bunch of questions about the panic attack, sleeping patterns, energy levels, etc. She began talking to me about how people find their fight with cancer to be difficult, but life after cancer to be more of a challenge. She said you have to get used to not having to report to doctors every other day, every other week, no more visitors, caretakers, medication, treatments, adjusting to and loving my new body, etc. And in trying to get back to "normal" everyone thinks you are back to your old self; your old normal. It's hard when everyone sees you and thinks, *She's better, back to her old self.* But, in reality, your normal is, in fact, different. And it is - patience for certain things; my tolerance for things, people and situations my energy; my strength. I'm getting adjusted to and acquainted with the new me and it can be challenging.

So, Robin is putting me back on Celexa and Ativan to help me deal with the anxiety. She wants me to talk with Stefanie and she referred me to a therapist. She pleaded with me to consider making an appointment. She knows my reluctance to speak with a therapist.

It has also helped to read through the Living Beyond Breast Cancer transcripts from different conferences. Everything I am experiencing emotionally is normal when I just thought I was being sensitive to different matters. I realize how emotional I would get any time cancer is brought up in any context. I felt I had to hide my emotions thinking someone would think I was being overly sensitive or that I wanted sympathy. Cancer was indirectly and directly a part of my life and it moves me in a way someone unaffected may never experience. I can't and won't apologize for that. Ever! I just have to understand that they don't understand it. Anyone having never experienced what I went through will never understand how cancer has affected or changed me. I can't feel guilty for feeling the way I feel, the moments I have, or the changes within me.

Cancer changes people in so many ways. I like how Ronnie Kaye put it in her February 24, 2007 conference on Moving on: Discovering your new normal. She said, "Time counts. Every second counts. The future was limitless before breast cancer. Breast cancer came along, and it was either do it now or possibly do it never. My time became more important to me. The choices that I made became more important to me." Those words couldn't be any truer.

My anxiety regarding cancer, after treatment, is normal. Julia Rowland spoke a lot about this at her May 15, 2008 conference on Moving Beyond Breast Cancer: From Treatment to Survivorship. Fears of recurrence, anniversary dates (surgeries, treatments, etc.), a smell, taste, person, environment of something that reminds you of treatment that can make you physically ill, other changes in my health that may bring concern, the heaviness of life's demands on top of trying to better me, fears of stress being related to recurrence. All of these are a part of my adjusting to my new normal and it can be challenging. Surprisingly though, the anniversary date of my surgery did not bother me as the anniversary date of my diagnosis. Thank God.

There are worries of being in intimate relationships. Will I lack in confidence? When someone special comes into my life, will I be comfortable with my new body? When someone new comes into my life, how and when do I discuss the changes my body went through? Will I be comfortable enough to talk about it and share myself with someone, exposing my new body? How will I handle the reaction?

February 13, 2009 Giving Back

I wanted to give back to those organizations that continue to do their best to assist families struggling to maintain while they face life altering situations. Thus far, I've donated to the following: Philabundance, Lupus Foundation of America, Crossing the Finish Line, Living Beyond Breast Cancer, American Cancer Society, Strong Kids –YMCA, MADD, Children's Hospital Foundation, March of Dimes, Trustees of UPenn and FORCE.

February 21, 2009 In the Family Conference at the Wellness Community of Philadelphia

What an emotional experience I shared with my mom as we watched Joanna Rudnick's film, *In the Family*. www.inthefamilyfilm.com. She not only touched on her story, but the story of others diagnosed with the gene, the decisions that must be made when tested positive for the gene and diagnosis of cancer. My mom and I laughed, cried, and were encouraged and inspired by the film. We reflected on how it feels to know or think of having passed the mutation onto our children. I am angry I carry this mutation that I may have passed onto my children. I am angry my children will one day have to consider getting tested for the gene, and if tested positive, the decisions they will be faced with to preserve their health.

I remember being tested positive for the gene and saying I would not remove anything unless I had to. I remember wondering if I removed my breasts/ovaries and never developed cancer. All that for nothing. When I look back, had I known just months after being tested positive that I would develop breast cancer, would my thoughts/feelings/actions been different? Perhaps. It's not easy waking up every morning: cancer, treatments, surgeries, recoveries, infections and medication being the first thing on your mind.

Being tested positive puts you through a whirlwind of emotions. It is mentally exhausting. Should I be proactive and remove this, save that? If I remove my ovaries, will I be thrown into menopause? Am I ok with no longer being able to have children? If I remove my breasts, will I be ok with the change in sensation, if there is any sensation left. What procedure is best for me? Which doctor is the best doctor for the procedure? How is his/her experience, history, skills, specialty, reputation, etc. There are so many concerns and choices to make regarding doctors, hospitals, finances, insurance coverage, procedures, and effects. Initially, I thought, *I have the gene, but I'm not claiming it. I'm going to keep living my life*. I had no idea how much there was to consider after being tested positive. I heard the doctors trying to counsel me, but I wasn't really listening to them. I couldn't hear them, my mind was racing. However, all of this didn't start with being tested positive. All of the decisions began with my mother's positive results: "Do I want to know if I am positive or negative? Do I want to know if I carry this gene? How will this test affect my life…me?"

Currently, the genetic test cost $3000. That's to test for all BRCA mutations. I have been told, if you have a family member who tested positive for a specific mutation (BRCA1, in my case) you can pay to have just that test done. It would cost less as well. My insurance covered the test in full because of my family's history. Just as they covered my mammograms since I was 25 years old. It's recommended to start mammograms at the age of 40. Heck, people younger and younger are being diagnosed with breast cancer. They need to reconsider the ages for mammograms.

The Abramson Cancer Center gave everyone a *Calming the Mind and Body- Meditation for Coping with Cancer* cd. It's very soothing and really calms the spirit. I plan to use this a couple of times a week to help me deal with anxiety. Uphs.upenn.edu/stress

February 23, 2009 Transvaginal Ultrasound Follow-up, Pre-Op with Rachael

Well, I was told the cyst, from the initial test, was on the left side, not the right. However, they did find a small cyst on the right and the one on the left looks ok. The doctor says it's probably something that is occurring during ovulation, but everything looks fine. They are going to review the test and I will hear from Robin about the results.

I met with Rachael directly after for pre-op. She went over my current meds, weight, height, allergies, blood pressure, etc. She asked if I've had any infections, injuries, etc. We went over pre-op instructions (no Motrin 7 days prior, no food or drink after midnight the night before; I'll get a call the day before with a time to come in, etc.). She informed me that Dr. Wu will be doing the nipples and making revisions (touch-ups) on each breast. She's also going to inject a steroid into the site where the jp drains were. Rachel says it seems I had a reaction to the plastic. This will soften the area. I will use the scar therapy pads after she does this. I was told it will be an hour long procedure and I'll be under intravenous anesthesia because of the touch-ups. Four weeks after the surgery, I will come in for the tattooing of my areola. Then, I should be done with plastic surgery, unless I want to make some changes, or have a problem with the implants (God forbid).

Dr. Wu said most likely my appointment will be in the afternoon, so nothing to eat after midnight. I'm going to STARVE! (Dramatic, I know). I think I am allowed clear liquids since I have a late appointment.

Maybe I'll distract myself from the anxiety and hunger by shopping for nipple tassels. Just kidding...

February 27, 2009 Aren't You the One...

The Church of Christian Compassion had a Women's Ministry doing a lesson on *The Lady and the Leaven*. The concept was that negativity, leaven, is not seen until the end result; once it has spread. My discipleship teacher, Andrea Wyche was the speaker and I love sitting under her word. So, I decided to go.

As I entered the class, Joanna, a discipleship sister from another class walks over to me. She reminds me that she sat behind me during discipleship graduation and remembers me in my scarf, frail and no eyebrows. She goes on to compliment me on how beautiful she thought I was. "Stunning", she says. She said I am the ideal product of a survivor who chose to submit to God and let Him take control of a distressing situation. She continued to say how beautiful I looked. I blushed, hugged and thanked her. She warmed my spirit and put a much needed smile on my face.

March 2, 2009 Déjà Vu

Ambler measured in at 8-10 inches of snow. The firm closed. Schools are closed. As I lie in bed, daytime television caught my attention. I began to feel queasy. I felt sickness sitting in my bedroom. That feeling took me back to when I was on disability, fighting for my health, taking a bunch of meds. I had to busy myself. I needed a distraction. I jumped up, started cleaning, made breakfast, and drowned myself in my homework. I wish I could get out to a movie or something, but the snow and cold forces me to stay in.

March 3, 2009 Tomorrow: Another Big Day

I'm nervous and excited. I think I'll take some before pictures since I've been healing so well. I'll consider taking pictures directly after surgery. I'm sure I'll be swollen and funny looking. I do want to take pictures after all the swelling has gone down.

The kids and I sat on my bed discussing tomorrow's procedure. Joey asked what the doctors planned to do. I told him they are doing the nipple reconstruction. My daughter makes a face, not sure how to process or visualize it. My son, on the other hand, with his pointers and thumbs in a pinching motion asks, "So, will they look like chocolate chip morsels?" OMGosh! I just fell out laughing.

I received the call from the hospital telling me to arrive at 7:25am. Great! I can get this done and over with early and enjoy the rest of my day off.

Decided to take some before pictures. My back and front are healing nicely. Dr. Wu says I look wonderful.

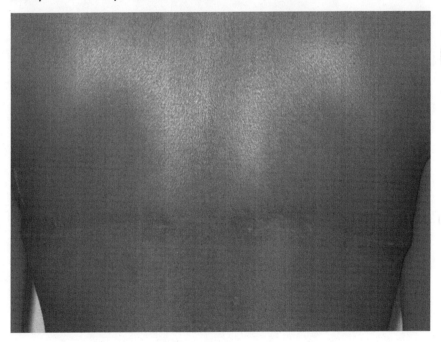

March 4, 2009 Getting Nipples

Being back in the SurgiCentre of the Perlman Building, I saw a lot of familiar faces from my surgery in November. Artis, the receptionist, was as comical as ever. Linda helped me get situated and did my vitals while admissions stopped over for a few signatures and a machine to process my copay. Another nurse came in to do my IV. She attached my bracelets: ID, medication allergy alert (I'm allergic to iodine) and warning bracelet stating no IV, BP or blood drawn from my right arm. I sat waiting for Dr. Wu to pop in. I dozed off for a few minutes feeling comfortable. When I woke, I asked Shan if she thought it strange that being back at the hospital - tubes in me, anticipating going in the OR and getting pumped with anesthesia - felt normal to me. I was so comfortable. No anxiety. Nothing. It was like "old times" (last year). It was as if I had gotten used to it and it was normal for me to be sitting waiting to be operated on.

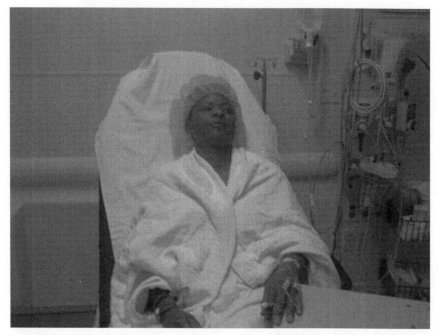

As I was being wheeled to the operating room, I told Shan to have a Stromboli, hot wings, mozzarella sticks, peach cobbler, sushi and a hoagie waiting for me. I was craving everything since I hadn't eaten. Of course I wouldn't eat all of that, nor would Shan buy all that. I'm just being a brat, wanting everything. "Eyes bigger than your stomach", my poppop used to say.

Everyone in the operating room - Dr. Wu, Jennifer, Anne, George, Dr. Gilbert and Dr. Daigle were so attentive. They walked me through everything they were doing: attaching monitors, giving me oxygen, putting the cuffs on my legs, covering me with the warm blankets, etc. Then I was told to take a few more deep breaths as Dr. Gilbert injected the anesthesia. I remember saying, "Oh...starting to get sleep..." I couldn't finish saying sleepy, I was out of it and the next thing I knew I was waking up in the recovery room, shivering. They brought me some more warm blankets. Artis even came back to give me a warm blanket to wrap around my neck. They went over my discharge instructions, gave me some crackers, apple juice and a prescription for a week's worth of Cephalexin (antibiotics). After a few minutes, I was ready to get dressed and get the heck out of there. They offered to wheel me down to the car, but I felt well enough to walk.

My son calls me from the school bus on his ride home. He asked how I was feeling now that I had my "nip nips". Ugh! He's going to be a boob man.

March 5, 2009 Another Unexpected Blessing, My Weight, Removing the Bandages

Got my Celexa, Tamoxifen and Ativan filled and there was no charge. The receipt said "miscellaneous discount". The manager verified that it was correct. So, I saved money on this month's prescriptions. Thank you Lord.

What the?! My weight is down to 137. What's going on? Ugh!

Well, I have nipples. Looks funny right now since they are still healing, but it's nice to see nipples again. I was able to take the bandages off 24 hours after the surgery so I was in the bathroom stall at work ripping that damn tape off of my skin. I'm sure that wasn't paper tape. Hurt so bad. So I cleaned the area and put gauze over them and went on about my business. I have to follow up with Dr. Wu in two weeks and I suppose two weeks after that I'll go in for the tattooing of my areola.

The following website offers information on how breast/nipple/ areola reconstruction are done. http://www.cancer.org/docroot/CRI/ content/CRI_2_6X_Breast_Reconstruction_After_Mastectomy_5. asp#Nipple_and_areola_reconstruction

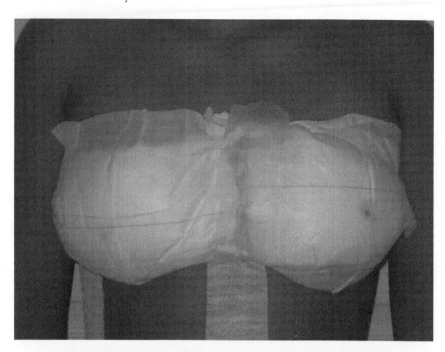

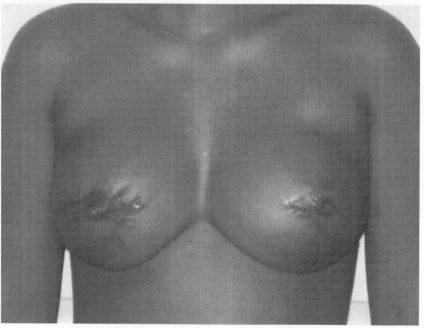

March 6, 2009 Shan Reflects On My Doctors

"I've noticed - when you're with Dr. Wu, it's how you look. She wants to make sure you like what you see. It appears as if she is really happy with your breasts. She leaned back, tilted her head and said, "They look good." I'm impressed with the way she makes decisions regarding your breasts. The decisions she makes today, may change tomorrow because your breasts change in the meantime - but you know she's always going to make the most educated decision at that time. She said you looked great.

When you're with Robin or Dr. Domchek, it's about how you feel - they also want to make sure you feel good about yourself."

Call from Dr. Wu's office

I received a call asking how I was feeling; if I removed the bandages and letting me know it's ok to shower, which I already did. I was told to drink plenty of fluids which was probably the reason for my dizzy spells and light headedness yesterday. I follow up with Dr. Wu March 16th.

March 9, 2009 Breathing Room Foundation

I received a letter today from the BRF similar to the one they sent for Christmas. They want to send Easter Baskets to the children. They asked me to supply a list of the things the kids enjoy. It will be delivered the week of Easter.

March 10, 2009 Decisions, Decisions

I can't have any more children. I think about my worries being a BRCA mutation carrier. It means a 50% chance of passing it to my offspring. I worry about the possibility of having passed it along to my children. I would be devastated.

I was thinking about the ovarian ultrasound and CA-125 ovarian test. I will have to do this every six months. Since I don't think I will be having any more children, time to consider removing my ovaries (Oophorectomy), which they highly recommend before I am 40 years old. My concern with removing my ovaries: taking away my option to bear more children, being thrown into menopause and losing a major source of estrogen. However, they suggest I not take estrogen (birth control) while on the Tamoxifen.

March 12, 2009 Breathing Room Foundation

The BRF left a box at my door with a label saying "Thinking of you, from the BRF." It was an assortment of Girl Scout cookies. Delicious treats! Thanks!

March 16, 2009 Follow-up with Dr. Wu

I had a follow-up with Dr. Wu. She removed the sutures and checked the healing progress of my nipples. She says they look really good. (And they do). One is a little more erect than the other, but she says they tend to flatten out a little anyway. She says she can make any corrections if I prefer. Dr. Wu told me to schedule for my tattoo (areolas) after the scabs have fallen off. I am able to put Neosporin on them and cover them with gauze.

Dr. Wu said she was done working on me and I wouldn't need to see her for six months. As I pouted from sadness that Dr. Wu would no longer be a part of my routine, she asked me for a hug and wished me well. She told me not to forget her and invited me to pop in for a visit when/if I was in the area. I promised I would as Dr. Wu was a major impact in my recovery from cancer. She is truly someone special to me.

March 20, 2009 A Survivor's Egoism?

As life throws obstacles my way, I wonder if I am wrong for feeling the way I tend to feel. *Why me?* I know I should find pleasure in and be grateful for the simplest things in life and life itself, something so precious, because it could have been taken away from me. So when I have to face the challenges of life and grow frustrated or discouraged, I feel guilty because I know I have been through worse. I question my faith because I tend to respond as if I have forgotten what God has brought me through; what He's done for me; how He's provided.

Then I think of how my life was spared. I know that He has work for me, and in that, I have a second chance at life and I want the best life has to offer. Not necessarily in a materialistic sense, but I've overcome a major ordeal; I want all my heart desires (God willing). Am I selfish for wanting things in my life to go smoothly; wanting what I want; what I feel I deserve? Or should I say God has brought me through such a dilemma and I should be satisfied with only the simplest things. I don't mean to seem greedy or ungrateful, but I don't want to seem as if I'm settling either. I want the world because my life has been spared. I feel a sense of entitlement after what I've been through. Oftentimes, I feel I should have to apologize for being me when, in fact, I shouldn't have to. I want the simplest things because they matter most and I want the finest things because I feel I deserve them. Is this not realistic? Is it selfish? Am I justified in feeling this way?

Lord, forgive me if I seem ungrateful at times. Forgive me if I get submerged in my feelings of entitlement. This has been a humbling experience. I thank you for all the blessings seen and unseen. I even thank you for the struggles as they help me appreciate the good all-the-more.

March 26, 2009 My Birthday, Italy…Finally!

I celebrated my 31st birthday two days ago. I was reminded a year ago of how I was being admitted into the hospital with an infection. The nurses came into my room carrying a plate of donuts and wished me happy birthday while expressing their sympathy as I was bringing in a milestone in the hospital.

When we (my sister and I) realized, a year ago, the trip had to be postponed, it seemed so far off. Now that I look back at what I've come through, the time went so fast. It just didn't seem that way while I was "in it." I felt like my battle with cancer would never end; like I would not make it.

I am in Tuscany on my dream vacation! Last year, a place I never thought I'd have the opportunity to see. I am here celebrating my birthday, life and good health. Thank you, God, for bringing me through. Thank you, Candice, my baby sis, for making my birthday, my 30th and 31st, a special one.

As we flew over snow covered mountains, leaving out of Frankfurt, Germany, heading to Florence, I looked down on the clouds and saw the beauty of God, from God; in God. I felt a sense of peace and was moved to say a simple, yet well deserved, "Thank you, Jesus."

Wine tasting in Tuscany

April 4, 2009 BRF, CFL, Seas It, Healing

David from the Breathing Room Foundation delivered the Easter baskets for each of the kids. They are beautiful baskets filled with chocolates, peeps, 5 gum (the kid's favorites) Rita's Water Ice coupons, a gift card to McDonalds, Regal Cinema gift cards, and a load of other goodies. I can't wait to give the kids their baskets this Easter. I need to send off another thank you card. This was another blessing.

Amber from CFL asked if I was willing to share my story for their Immeasurable Joy Page. I felt honored and moved to share my story. I typed a page about my battle and how CFL has blessed my family and included pictures from our respite in Ventnor, NJ.

I also received an email from Amanda at Seas It. They are coming up on their 5 year fundraiser this July and want to give out information packets on how Seas It helps cancer patients. She also invited me to the event which marks the 5 year anniversary of Seas It and the date that Todd, her husband, and the one who inspired the evolution of Seas It, was told he had six months to live. He's still alive and doing well. Amanda asked if I could write a brief testimonial of my experience with Seas It. I told her I would be honored to share my story.

Areola tattooing

Called Dr. Wu's office. I'm scheduled to get the areola tattooing done May 6th. I was told it should take about one hour. This chapter in my life is coming to a close.

April 13, 2009 Scar Therapy Pads

The pads have done such a wonderful job on my back. I started using the pads on my breast to see if the scars would lighten up. I am not extremely worried about it. I'm sure the tattooing of my areolas will cover some of the scarring, but I figured it wouldn't hurt to try. I was lucky and found the store brand pads at CVS. I haven't had any luck finding the name brand pads at CVS or Rite Aid since the first time I purchased them.

May 6, 2009 Areola Tattoo with Yelena

This procedure took about an hour. It is literally like getting a tattoo. I can't explain how it felt. Not quite like getting a tattoo because I don't have much feeling in my breasts, but there was a moment I felt a little discomfort in the left breast.

Yelena took out a stencil of different size circles so I could choose the size areola I wanted. Then she placed a blotch of different shades of brown on my breast to match a color just right for my complexion.

Afterwards, she cleaned the area, drew her circle then proceeded to tattoo the area.

After she finished, she cleaned both breasts, covered with Vaseline and put gauze over them to protect my clothing from the slight bleeding. She said I should come back three more times for a retouch because the color can fade approximately 30% to 50% during the initial tattoo. Color will appear lighter after peeling (approximately 4-5 days after procedure). I can expect dryness similar to chapped lips. Vaseline has to be applied in the morning and evening. Things to be avoided are hot tubs, pools, Jacuzzis and rubbing the area with anything abrasive. I didn't need any pain medication, but was recommended to take Tylenol if I experienced any discomfort.

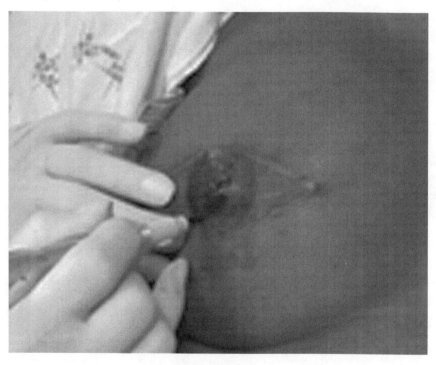

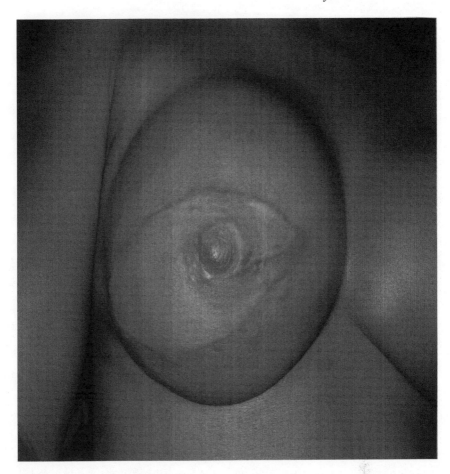

June 1, 2009 Breathing Room
Foundation - Summer Program

Eileen from the BRF sent me a letter saying they'd like to provide some enjoyment for their families in hopes of giving the kids something to talk about when they return to school. They offer zoo passes, museum passes, blockbuster gift certificates and more. I filled out the form and received a free lane bowling party for five people at Thunderbird Bowling Center in Willow Grove. It covers up to five people for two hours of unlimited bowling, free shoe rental, pizza and soda. We also received four passes to Dorney Park and three movie passes. The kids will be so excited. I just sent the BRF another thank you for continuing to be a blessing in the lives of those struggling and overcoming battles with Cancer.

June 3, 2009 Second Tattooing

This one was a little more uncomfortable than the first. The pain traveled to my arms. Tylenol helped to ease the discomfort. Not sure if I want to do any more. It's suggested that I come back once or twice more. I'll consider.

October 10, 2009 Sisters Surviving Breast Cancer – Philadelphia Hilton

American Cancer Society and Women of Faith and Hope hosted the 14th Annual Sisters Surviving Breast Cancer event. To my surprise, I saw many familiar faces. Some I didn't realize had their own battles with cancer. I sat at the table and couldn't stop looking around the room at all the many faces of cancer: survivors, caregivers, supporters, doctors, educators. I felt a sense of home; like I was amongst family. I could relate to all of these women.

We started with continental breakfast and networking. There was candle lighting in honor and remembrance and many educational sessions. I attended the stress management workshop which was very relaxing and informative. We ended with lunch, door prizes and a fashion show.

October 21, 2009 The End of My Story?

People are always asking at what point does my book (story) end. My answer is it never does.

As I revisit the *BrcaAnalysis* information I received after my gene test, I reflect on the chances of cancer recurring. Because I had breast cancer, my chances for ovarian cancer are 15%. The possibility of breast cancer recurring after five years is 27%. As a gene (mutation) carrier, I am forced to make decisions to increase the chances for early detection and/or decrease my chances of cancer recurring (e.g. do I, or do I not, have my ovaries removed). If I remember correctly, there is an 80% lifetime chance of cancer recurring because I am BRCA1 positive.

Having had reconstruction with implants, I hope to not have problems with my implants (rupture/leakage). Because I have silicone implants, I have to be mindful of any changes in the shape of my breasts which is a sign of leakage. I learned that an MRI will be scheduled periodically to assure there are no problems with the implants. The MRI can detect leaks in silicone implants. I also have to keep in mind that most implants will need to be replaced every 15-20 years.

I feel honored and compelled to walk for the cause, engender awareness; donate for research and financial assistance, attend special events, conferences, workshops and seminars. I am also invited to 2009 holiday, acknowledgement and educational events given by the various programs that have assisted me throughout my season with cancer.

I keep saying I need to follow up with Dr. Wu about a tingly sensation in my breasts when someone rubs my back. Not arousing/stimulating at all. It just feels…weird. I hate for someone to touch my back sometimes. On occasion, it feels more sensitive than others. And, at times, my breasts itch. It drives me crazy! I'm still adjusting to my scars; my reminder of what my body had to endure. It's an adjustment feeling sexy, to me, with my "battle scars". I also continue the fight to regain my strength and energy.

I am learning and growing comfortable with the new me, ("my new normal"), and so is everyone around me. At the time of diagnosis, the survivor is different. The survivor is different with each phase of fighting cancer - treatment, surgery, complication, healing, going into survivorship, etc.

All that to say, as I continue to adjust to the many changes that my body has gone through; changes I've gone through mentally; the chances of cancer returning; my kid's future considerations of getting the gene test; how can I say my story has come to an end?

Although my story does not end, this chapter in my life has come to a close. My journal for this season has come to a close. If you have any questions, or want to share your story - I'd be honored to hear from you. Email me: Whoneedshair@live.com Or friend me on Facebook: facebook.com/profile.php?id=100001039583711 twitter.com/lovetk78 linkedin.com/pub/tyesha-love/21/72b/a94

Frequently Asked Questions from Friends and Family
(Answers not based on professional advice, but personal experience)

How has this experience changed your perspective on life?

Life and our time are brief yet so precious. We must make the best of each day as tomorrow is not promised. We've all heard these and know how true they are. Many people take a lot for granted and an experience, such as mine, will shift all of that. I've learned to appreciate more of the simple pleasures that life has to offer; to cherish those close and dear to me. I am more aware of the negativity around me and do my best to not to get caught up in it. I try to avoid mentally/spiritually/ physically/emotionally draining people and situations. I've learned to wean out the things and people that have been negative, insignificant and inconsistent and devote my time and energy to only those things and people that are beloved. I've learned to not hesitate to do the things I want to do as the opportunity may not present itself again. I've learned to not have any regrets, harbor bitterness, hatred, anger or envy. Life is too short. They are not healthy for me nor are they worth my time. I've learned to lean and trust on the Lord more than I ever have. I call on Him for strength in my weakness, patience in my haste, courage in my fears, trust in my doubt, understanding in my bewilderment, healing in my infirmities, peace in my chaos, light in my darkness and strengthening of my faith.

Would I go through this (surgery/treatment) again?

My first reaction was NO! It was a horrible experience. I suffered too many side effects from chemo: nausea, vomiting, fatigue, hair loss, mouth sores (taste changes), nail discoloration, aches/pains, depression, weakness, and chemo brain. Then, I keep thinking, I need to beat this and be here for my children and other loved ones. I need to beat this because there is so much more I have/want to do in life. I have to beat this because God has a plan for me. I have to beat this so I can be a testimony for someone else.

For a plethora of information about breast cancer symptoms, diagnosis, treatments, and side effects, I found the following website to be helpful. http://www.breastcancer.org/

What are some of the emotional phases you went through?

Beginning at the time of diagnosis, I went through a phase of complete numbness. I felt alone in this moment as if I were the only person in the world who's gotten a cancer diagnosis. That was the first phase. I was in disbelief. I felt like I was stuck in a bad dream and couldn't wake up. I was in a complete daze. Next, I went through a period of denial. I wanted to ask the doctor to double check charts, do another test, anything. They had to be wrong. Then, I accepted that this was my fate. I told myself that I was going to find out all I could about my diagnosis and my options. After awhile, anger set in. Why did I have to endure such a plight? Why me? Then faith kicked in. I told myself to leave it all in God's hands as he would see me through. I had moments of doubt and fear, especially when I got the infections, was hospitalized or when I would get sick from the treatments. I wondered, "Will I get through this, can I get through this; am I going to die?"

I probably could have asked for medical counseling during these times, but instead, I leaned on my spiritual family. They were beneficial in keeping me positive and strong in faith. I also shifted my negative energy by doing things I found pleasure in.

How was the experience dealing with social workers?

The hospital's social workers were exceptionally informative regarding programs, assistance, counseling and support groups. I was reluctant to seek counseling for several reasons. Although I should have sought help in my time of depression, I loathed the idea of "building a new relationship" in order to feel comfortable opening up to a therapist. I shut down pretty bad anyway so I didn't want to talk to anyone. I knew with the distance I traveled for treatments, I could not see burning more gas to travel several times a week to sit with someone for an hour. Co-pays were adding up and it made no sense for me to add more medical bills on top of those I already accumulated with only 60% of my income coming in.

Like with every other decision you have to make, you must ask yourself if it's the best thing for you. You cannot be pressured into seeking counseling. Consider that it may be beneficial to you, but you have to want the help. I managed to find positive ways to channel my energy. I forced myself out of bed. Once I was showered, I felt like I could take on the day. I tended to my plants, painted their pots and went on small outings with the children. I always had company full of buoyancy and great laughs. We'd order take-out, have drinks, share laughs, watch movies, play games and/or relax and enjoy some music.

I am blessed to have so many people in my life that care for me. I was able to go to family/friends to cry, vent, celebrate, etc.

What do my breasts feel like with the expanders in place?

Hard! I have no feeling in them so they just serve the purposes of looking nice under my clothes. The idea of having "breasts" was comforting. I'm anxious about seeing the final results. I have so much faith and confidence in Dr. Wu's work.

How do we comfort you?

Allow me to feel what I'm feeling. Let me cry, scream, praise...Sit with me in silence when there are no words to be said. Encourage me when I'm down. Make me laugh. Help in any way with the kids or household chores. Get me out of the house, even if it's just for a walk in the park, a matinee, a cup of coffee, or to read a book for an hour at the local library or café.

As the patient, it's also important to remember to not neglect or reject the feelings of those close to you. They too may need to talk about their feelings, thoughts, fears, concerns regarding you and your diagnosis, treatment, recovery, etc. Allow loved ones to see you when you are vulnerable. They will better understand you, what you need, what you are feeling.

How do we know with all that you are doing, it won't come back?

I don't. Well, I had my breast (tissues) removed so there is no where for cancer to attack in the breasts. The chemo, in my case, was to prevent any (and hopefully all) cancer cells from multiplying, although it can harm healthy cells. "It's an insurance policy," Robin says, "to get what [cancer cells] may have gotten away." It's to kill those cancer cells. However, I am positive for the BRCA1 gene, which puts me at higher risks for developing a cancer. So, I'm more at risk, although I am not claiming that either, for developing another type of cancer (cervical, ovarian, endometrial, pancreatic, lung, etc.). Chemotherapy is used for a number of reasons.

Scott Hamilton has a great website that offers a substantial amount of information about chemotherapy. http://www.chemocare.com/

Will certain foods compromise your recovery?

The only time food became an issue was during chemo. I was told to avoid acidic, spicy, greasy, fried and salty food; caffeine and alcohol. The concerns were regarding the mouth sores/stomach upset. When I went through periods of nausea and vomiting, I would snack on crackers and sip on broth or soup (Wonton soup from the local Chinese store was my favorite). I would keep plastic bags in my car, pocketbook, book bag, and pockets of outfits. They came in handy when the nausea snuck up on me.

Holly Clegg & Gerald Miletello, M.D. wrote a book titled *Eating Well Through Cancer, Easy recipes & recommendations during and after treatment* (chemo). I really liked this book as it provided quick, nutritious, tasteful recipes.

Can an illness (cold/infection) I have, compromise your recovery?

Yes, mostly while on chemo. A chemo patient's immune system weakens which makes it harder to fight colds/infections or heal (from surgery, injury, etc.). When I would have visitors, it was mandatory that they sanitize their hands before coming into my bedroom.

Are you able to drink (alcoholic beverages)?

YES! Although I was instructed to avoid alcohol while on chemo. I needed one every once in awhile. Especially a glass of wine or something the night before surgery. However, while on chemo and for some time after I finished with chemo, alcohol and some foods, taste "funny." It's common for taste changes to occur in chemo patients so I did not enjoy apple martinis (my favorite) as much. So I stuck to wine.

How big are your breasts going to be?

The size I want. Lol. Actually, I'm aiming for a full B, small C. The perfect and perky size I was before I had children. Now, to get ideas for the nipple and areola size. Hmm, maybe the nipple the size of a pencil eraser, or a tad bit smaller? The areola the size of the bottom of a yogurt cup. I don't know...something to consider. Hmmm...

Does it become annoying or overwhelming having people ask you about your experience, asking about cancer, treatments, seeing advertisements for cancer awareness, treatment centers, etc.

No. It can be emotional at times, but never a nuisance. I do not mind people asking about my experience because I have seen how cancer affected people close to me and I have had my own battle; therefore, I can educate others, the afflicted, newly diagnosed, caregivers, loved ones or the curious, based on my experience. When people come to me regarding the various programs, advertisements for treatment centers, etc., it gratifies me to know that there are individuals, organizations and companies who are supporting survivors, their loved ones and caregivers; continuously offering assistance; seeking to be educated and empowered; fighting for a cure.

How has this experience affected your children? (From Shan's perspective)

In the beginning (right after you were diagnosed), the kids seemed to be fine. They were fine. I guess because we did our best to keep things as normal as possible. School, homework, afterschool camp, TEAM, T.E.A.L., cleaning rooms on the weekend, etc., we succeeded with the daily routine -- doing everything like we had been. It wasn't until your week long hospital stay (March 24 - March 29) that I noticed a change in the kids.

One day, I recall going to pick up the kids from camp and they were concerned if you were going to ever come home. Not too long after that, Joseph started to rebel. He began to lash out in very negative ways......acting out in school, at home........ it was as if he had no way/where to vent. Once at the hospital, and after he saw you, Joseph made a complete turn-around. He no longer felt as if he was going to lose his mother. You made him feel safe, secure, and most of all LOVED.

Taylor acted out too, however, but not to the extent to which Joseph did. Her daily routine didn't fall short as much as Joseph's. Perhaps she kept more of her fears and feelings inside. But as with Joseph, once she saw you in the hospital and felt your loving arms around her and heard your voice...........she too was comforted in a way no one else could comfort her -- except her mother.

What is chemo brain and did you suffer from it?

Yes, I did and it can be quite frustrating. Chemo brain is a term used for forgetfulness/trouble concentrating/trouble multi-tasking. It's a "brain fog/cloudiness". Shan would notice, after awhile, I would ask the same questions over and over. I would forget things I'd done or events that happened. I would forget appointments even though they were of great importance. Both websites below offer information on chemo brain, what it is and how it can be managed.

http://www.cancer.org/docroot/MBC/content/MBC_2_3x_Chemobrain.asp or

http://www.cancer.org/docroot/MBC/content/MBC_2_3x_Chemobrain.asp?sitearea=MBC

How inspirational was it, knowing that your mom made it through this ordeal multiple times herself?

Knowing my mom had three battles with cancer, and won, was comforting that I too could/would overcome this challenge. She provided me with comfort, guidance, information and wisdom to make it through my dilemma. Her experiences and the experiences of each woman in my family, who was diagnosed with cancer, were the foundation of which some of my decisions were made. Their stories and experience are my education and inspiration. They give me hope.

How did your children react when you told them you were sick?

They asked if it was the same thing Noni (my mom; their grand mom) had. I believe, in their minds, since their grandmother was now doing well, they figured, mom would be ok. I don't think they truly understood my diagnosis. At least, not until my week long hospital stay. That scared them more than anything. My daughter asked if I would die or if I would get better. My son wondered if I could still get on roller coaster rides with him at Great Adventure. Seems as long as everything remained "normal" for them, they did well.

The National Cancer Institute has a *Guide for Teens* titled *When your Parent has Cancer.*

What was most challenging during this season?

There were mental, emotional, spiritual and physical challenges. Besides surgeries, complications, treatments, hair loss and finance issues, there were many things that were challenging for me.

One of the things I found most difficult was losing a sense of self. This is where I give thanks to all those loved ones who helped me "pick up the slack." At different times, I allowed myself to get so mired by cancer; I could not focus on giving my children the proper care and attention. I lacked energy and lost interest in tending to my home (chores). I allowed myself to get so consumed with my situation I forgot that people close to me needed help dealing with the situation just as well. I forgot about my strength and will to face head on this bump in my road. I allowed cancer to become everything when it was only a small part of me. I had moments I was lost in cancer; forgetting cancer did not define who I was.

The other challenge is the affect that cancer has on relationships; friendships. I think of my dear friend, Shan; all she's done and all I put her through. She was the closest to me and the only one I allowed to see me vulnerable. At times, I loathed her sternness when it came to me taking my pills; getting me out of bed; trying to make the best of the day. I fought with her often, when it came to pill time; wound cleaning time; bathing and dressing for the day. I took my anger and frustrations out on her, unintentionally...regretfully. I was so mean, at times. It takes a special person to tolerate some of the callousness I put on her. She understood that what I was enduring was distressful. She did not take it personally; fought me back and continued to do what I needed done, keeping my best interest at heart. Rare will you find a gem like her. She cared for, supported and loved me unconditionally. There were times I could tell she was irritated with me. I'm sure the times I mistreated her did not help. However, she remained loyal to our friendship; to me and continued to do what she believed was best and what needed to be done (probably while neglecting her own needs).

This leads me to think about caregiver burnout. Shan devoted her time (day and night) to caring for me, without remuneration. I think of the mental, emotional and physical exhaustion she must have felt at times while caring for me through each process. How easy it must be for a caregiver to say, "This is too much. I can't deal with this anymore." and just walk out on it all. People do it all of the time: Spouses, significant others, friends, associates, and family members. Being a caregiver can take its toll. Caregivers need just as much love, support and encouragement as the person to whom they provide care.

Inspiration

I realized that God is at work in my life. I am no saint. God has his work cut out with me. However, I know who I belong to. I remind myself that "all things are for the good for those who believe in Him and are called according to His purpose". Maybe it's not time for me to fully understand His plan for me, but I know I need to surrender to His calling. When I am feeling challenged in my faith; when I am ready to give up; when I need a reminder that I am a child of God; when I need to feel a sense of hope; when I fall short; when I am afraid; when I am discouraged; when I need relief from pain, depression and/or sorrow; when I need comfort; when I feel alone, these are just a few scriptures that helped me through. I could have just written out the verses, but take it upon yourself to open up the Word and apply it to your life; your situation.

PSALM 118:24	PROVERBS 3:5
PROVERBS 17:22	NEHEMIAH 8:10
JOHN 14:1	PSALM 34:4
PSALM 55:22	MATTHEW 8:26
PSALM 121	MATTHEW 6:25-34
JOHN 14:1-4	PHILIPPIANS 4:6-7
ROMANS 5:3-5	2 CORINTHIANS 12:9-10
JAMES 1:2-3	GENESIS 50:20
ROMANS 5:3-4	JOHN 14:1
PSALM 27:1	DEUTERONOMY 31:6
PSALM 23	MARK 9:24
PSALM 56:8	MATTHEW 6:9-13

A list of some of the music that fills my spirit with joy and ease

- India Arie - Intro: Loving, Good Morning, I Am Not My Hair
- Earth Wind and Fire - That's the Way of the World
- Sam Cooke - Just another day, He'll Make a Way, Be with me Jesus, Touch of the Hem of His Garment, I'm so Glad (trouble don't last always), Jesus Wash Away my Troubles
- Sweetback - You Will Rise
- Stevie Wonder - (cd) Songs in the Key of Life, You Will Know
- Kirk Franklin - Songs for the Storm, Vol. 1
- Kirk Franklin - Declaration (This is it)
- Yolanda Adams - The Battle is the Lord's
- Shirley Caesar - He's Working It Out
- Yolanda Adams - Victory
- Yolanda Adams - Be Blessed
- Nina Simone - Here Comes the Sun
- Nina Simone - Feelin Good
- Billie Holiday - Smile
- James Blunt - You're Beautiful
- Maze w/ Frankie Beverly - Happy Feeln's
- Musorgsky - Promenade
- Sweetback - You Will Rise
- The Five Stairsteps - O-O-H Child
- Vivaldi: Violin Concerto in E Major, 'The Spring', I
- Musorgsky - Polish Ox-Cart
- Lionel Richie - All Night Long
- Mozart - A Little Nights Music, I
- Maze w/ Frankie Beverly - Golden Time of Day
- Etta James - Tough Mary
- Fiona Apple - Extraordinary Machine

Inspirational Messages

Dove (candy)Promise Messages from the candy wrappers:

- "Dream as if you'll live forever. Live as if you'll die tomorrow."

- "Patience is a virtue."

- "Count your blessings not your worries."

- "Remind yourself that it's okay not to be perfect."

Fortune Cookie Message:

- "Live, think and act for today. Tomorrow may be too late.

Inspirational Books:

- *The Holy Bible*
- *Purpose Driven Life, Purpose Driven Life Journal* – Rick Warren

Gifts I Received While in the Hospital for Mastectomy

Shan - The best of care, love, support and encouragement
The Firm - A beautiful bouquet of flowers
The Firm's Securities Department - A beautiful bouquet of flowers
Julie - (My travel agent) - bouquet of flowers
El - Roses
Sherri - Carnations
Tamarah - Basket of flowers
Donald - Fruit flowers and stuffed bear
Sherell - Card, monetary gift and a visit (something she struggled with
as she felt it difficult to see me in this condition) Thanks girl. Seeing
you lifted my spirits.
Michelle - Card from the job signed by everyone
Dad - Balloons and ice cream
Sharrie - White cranberry juice. I love the stuff
Discipleship class - Fruit basket and cards
Meah - Photo Album for my trip to Italy, Orchid
Bonnie - Soup for the women's soul
Jackie - Italian cook book, journal for Italy
Charles, Kelly, Salihya, Michele – Fruit Flowers, balloons

Additional Websites/Books/Associations/ etc...that you may find helpful. I did.

There is a plethora of information on cancer, treatments, side effects, etc. It can become quite overwhelming. To keep from getting inundated, I weaned out information packets and brochures that repeated information and kept only those I found relevant and helpful. Here are just a few I'd like to mention:

Books & Pamphlets

- The National Cancer Institute has a Guide for Teens titled *When your Parent has Cancer*
- Emedguides.com: *A Patient Guide to Breast Cancer Resources on the Internet*
- Breastcancer.org: *Your Guide to the Breast Cancer Pathology Report*
- Chhealthysystem.com: *Hospital Prayers and Scripture*
- American Cancer Society can give a listing of support groups in your county
- Living Beyond Breast Cancer, Insight Newsletter
- University of Pennsylvania's *Genetic Testing for Breast & Ovarian Cancer Risk* – Informational Guide

Websites

- http://www.breathingroomfoundation.org/Home_Page.php
- http://www.lbbc.org/
- http://www.crossingthefinishline.org/?fb_page_id=21619701381&
- http://www.crossingthefinishline.org/sailor-detail.asp?id=11 (TL's sailor story)
- http://www.BRCAnow.com/
- Profile on Dr. Liza Wu http://www.uphs.upenn.edu/surgery/faculty/lcw.html
- http://www.chemocare.com/
- http://www.youngsurvival.org/

- http://www.breastcancer.org/
- **TLC Tender Loving Care** is a not-for-profit patient service of the American Cancer Society intended to make coping easier for women experiencing hair loss due to chemotherapy, radiation treatment or surgery. http://www.tlcdirect.org/
- American Cancer Society http://www.cancer.org/docroot/home/index.asp?level=0
- http://www.mayoclinic.com/health/cancer-treatment/CA00044 Chemo Brain
- Important Information for Reconstruction Patients about Mentor MemoryGel Silicone Gel-Filled Breast Implants http://www.mentorcorp.com/breastsurgery/reconstruction/index.htm
- Hats, turbans and wigs for hair loss. For cancer, chemotherapy, alopecia, trichotillomania and other medical patients. http://www.headcovers.com/
- "Recognizing the Warning Signs of Breast Cancer" Susan G. Komen for the Cure www.Komen.org
- "Five Questions You should Ask Before Supporting a Corporate Cause-Related Marketing Program" Susan G. Komen for the Cure www.Komen.org
- www.inthefamilyfilm.com
- http://www.ovariancancer.org/